FROM "HUH?" TO "HURRAY!"

Righting Your Creative Writing

Stephanie Stiles

University Press of America,® Inc.
Lanham · Boulder · New York · Toronto · Plymouth, UK

Copyright © 2010 by
University Press of America,® Inc.
4501 Forbes Boulevard
Suite 200
Lanham, Maryland 20706
UPA Acquisitions Department (301) 459-3366

Estover Road
Plymouth PL6 7PY
United Kingdom

All rights reserved
Printed in the United States of America
British Library Cataloging in Publication Information Available

Library of Congress Control Number: 2010936057
ISBN: 978-0-7618-5336-7 (paperback : alk. paper)
eISBN: 978-0-7618-5337-4

∞™ The paper used in this publication meets the minimum
requirements of American National Standard for Information
Sciences—Permanence of Paper for Printed Library Materials,
ANSI Z39.48-1992

For Eric, Nicholas, and, now, Allison

Contents

Preface	vii
Acknowledgements	ix
Introduction	xi
Chapter 1: Getting Started	1
Chapter 2: Focusing on Details	5
Chapter 3: Constructing a Setting	9
Chapter 4: Building Character	13
Chapter 5: Knowing Your Character	17
Chapter 6: Creating Conflict	21
Chapter 7: Speaking the Truth	25
Chapter 8: Motivating the Agents	29
Chapter 9: Finding Your Point of View	33
Chapter 10: Relying on the Unreliable	37
Chapter 11: Taking the Time	41
Chapter 12: Choosing the Words	45
Chapter 13: Structuring Symbols	49
Chapter 14: Making Meaning	53
Chapter 15: Mastering Irony	57
Chapter 16: Addressing Your Audience	61
Chapter 17: Reviewing the Work	65
Chapter 18: Revising Your Work	73
Chapter 19: Polishing Your Manuscript	77
Chapter 20: Being a Writer	81
Epilogue	85
Index	87

PREFACE

Most of us have been writing for a while. A long while. Probably since before kindergarten. So why, after all that time and all those years, do we still find ourselves studying and practicing one of the most basic, elemental skills available to us? Easy. To get better at it. And that is why this book is here for you, presumably in your hands right now. While all of us already know how to inscribe ink marks and letters on a page, those of us who truly wish to be *writers* want to know how to transfigure those scratchings into something far greater than mere component parts of the alphabet.

So, this book is designed to help, by putting to use the most important tool of all when it comes to writing: you. Contained within are various exercises and suggestions, chosen with you in mind. These are brief assignments, but each can easily be developed into a much longer, fuller, self-contained piece. The structure and intent of this text is meant to provide you with a basis from which to grow your writing–regardless of the level of your experience as a writer. Even the greatest writers can benefit from further practice, and this text offers exactly that. By using this book and following the exercises included here, you will be able to focus on specific elements of your craft and improve them. Writing is not a mindless art; it requires attention, focus, and, if not love, at least, devotion and admiration. But it also has to be engaging, satisfying, and fun. I hope this book makes it all of those.

Whether you're an instructor or a student, a poet or a novelist, a professional or a beginner, this book can assist you in the process of fulfilling your greatest potential. The chapters and the suggested assignments may be completed in successive order, or they can be studied on an as-needed basis; it doesn't change the general intent of the text, which is to get you to write. The exercises are infinitely adaptable, so you should feel free to alter them in any way that assists you in your creation. The important thing is to write, and with these exercises, that should become an easier, more habitual undertaking for you.

These chapters cover the essentials of getting your thoughts down on paper and getting you prepared to share these with the world at large. This book does not touch on the process of publication, manuscript production, query-letter writing, or marketing; what this book focuses on is making you the best writer you can be. So, read on and then get started. With a little bit of practice, you'll be able to unlock a whole new world–for you and for your readers. And the response you get will jump *from "huh?" to "hurray!"*

ACKNOWLEDGEMENTS

Thank you to Dominican College for all the friendship and support I've received during these fifteen years. In particular, thank you to the English Department and all its members, past and present, for making this, and so much more, possible for me. I'd also like to give a special thank you to my Creative Writing students, who are the real inspiration for this book. And, lastly, thank you to my family for their love and encouragement.

INTRODUCTION

So, you want to be a writer? Well, this workbook should help you out. Whether you're a total novice or an old pro, the exercises that follow have been designed for and used by writers just like you in order to assist in the process of being and becoming a better writer. Maybe you're a poet; maybe you write memoirs; maybe you're working on a screenplay or a novel–well, whatever your genre, whatever your medium, the exercises included here will help you find your voice, strengthen your talents, and develop your confidence. They do not pertain to any one type of writing, but, rather, these simple assignments allow you, as the author, to adapt them to and incorporate them in whatever mode you choose. And, perhaps more importantly to some of you, they'll help provide you with a basic starting point, because, let's face it, a blank page (or screen) can often seem less like an opportunity than an obstacle unless you have the means to fill it.

However, before you get started, there are a few things you should keep in mind. Like, for example, the fact that writing is democratic–a skill available to all of us regardless of age, class, wealth, or gender; it isn't some sort of obscure ideal that is unattainable to the great masses huddled beneath its printed pages. Writing is open to anyone willing to undertake it; but, like all skills, it needs to be practiced and honed and exercised regularly. You can't pick up a pen some random day–or start tapping at your keyboard–and expect the words to just materialize in brilliant and entertaining ways for you and your audience, any more than my seven-year-old son could pick up a bat for the first time and start swinging for the Yankees. It takes some time to develop if you want to get it right. Writing may be cathartic, it may be fun, it may even be necessary for you–but, above all, it must be practiced. And the exercises in this workbook will assist you in your training.

You should also keep in mind that, having bought (or at least read–but I really hope *bought*) this book, you probably already take your writing seriously. As such, henceforth, you should consider yourself "a writer." Until you begin to see and understand yourself in this role, no one else will believe it. Think of yourself as "a writer," describe yourself as "a writer," comport yourself as "a writer." You may be many other things–daughter, student, friend, football player–but always remember that you are, simultaneously, a writer. So *be* a writer.

And, as such, writers are always at work. You may be at a party, on a date, waiting tables, riding the subway, or sitting in class when you overhear a line of dialogue, an artful turn of phrase, or an intriguing speech pattern. Write it down. At the grocery store or your brother's band practice you may glimpse the exact character for your next story. Write it down. How did you feel when your girlfriend dumped you in your own fraternity's basement, or when your professor forced you to answer one of his ridiculously open-ended questions in front of class? Write it down. See an ugly shirt? Write it down. Hear a great song? Write it down. Particularly gross hamburger? You got it: write it down. Writing may be a labor of love for you–or it may just be a labor–but, either way, as a writer, your job is to put the tiniest elements of life onto paper for the world to see and take notice of. So do it.

This is where the practice comes in. As you well know (those of you who've ever started a research paper at four o'clock in the morning on the day that it's due), it isn't enough simply to put some words on a page and send them out to the public. There are certain rules and expectations we have to adhere to if we are going to express ourselves effectively. I wouldn't run into my local A&P wearing a toga, top hat, and go-go boots, even though that would technically constitute an outfit; people would avoid or ridicule me for my sartorial middle-finger. Well, similarly, there are guidelines to the written word, as well. There are, of course, things like grammar (which you've probably been learning since before kindergarten) and word choice and spelling–the tools of a writer's trade. But, more important (and far more evasive) are the nuanced elements of style, precision, clarity, and meaning. Why are you writing this? What's the take-away here? Is there a point to all this? A good writer has these answered. I had a friend in college who would talk to me endlessly. Seriously, her stories endured without cessation. There were times when I picked up my phone to order pizza, and I'd find her mid-sentence, mid-way through story she'd started the week before. God, how I wish she'd had this book. Because, let's face it: everybody tells stories. They're just not always good stories. Ever talk to a little kid on the phone? There's your evidence. This workbook will help you learn what goes in, and–*way* more importantly–what *stays out* of a piece of good writing. And that requires practice. The exercises contained within can be done in isolation, or they can be done progressively; they can be done as solo missions, or they can be done with a larger group (your class or a writers' group). Use them however they most benefit you, but do not spend all your time choosing an exercise and then running out of time to do the writing. The point here is to do the exercises, in whatever order or method you find helpful, and to keep on doing them. Write, write, write.

Of course, there's also the audience to consider. And you will have an audience. You're not, after all, reading this book in order to write more clearly in your diary, are you? This means that, at some point, you intend for someone else to read your work. Well, remember something important here: you're not going to be there when every fan of yours picks up your *Collected Poems* or your great American novel. If they don't get what you're saying, they're not going to be able to ask you to explain it. If you think the main character's shirt needs to be described more clearly, you can't just lean over your reader's shoulder and say, "I mean, really, it was more like the color of the walls in the cafeteria," or "It's supposed to look just like that shirt that Matt wore on Friday night." So, although you have as many opportunities to get it right as you need, it's only the final one that matters to your reader. That is why many of the exercises included here call on you either to share with an audience or to act, yourself, as an audience, asking questions that you, as the author, will have to know how to answer.

Creative writing is a boundless pursuit. You can have as much (or little) fun with it as you choose. But you should always take it and yourself seriously. And you should always strive to improve upon yourself. You can get better. In fact, you should get better. All it takes is a little dedication and some practice. So, sit yourself down, crack open the first exercise, and get writing. And then don't stop.

CHAPTER ONE:

GETTING STARTED

Okay, so now you're a writer. Feel different? You should–you've just claimed membership within the creative community. Even if you haven't put down word one, you have taken an important step in being and becoming a better writer: you have identified yourself *as a writer*. Who is in this community? Anyone who composes, reads, critiques, suggests, or contributes to the production of the written word; in short, it's pretty much wide open. More important, however, than identifying who *they* are is to identify who *you* are. You have to find that elusive thing that all writers need: your voice. But what is a "voice?" To find the answer to this, all you have to do is sit down and listen. Although you may not know what your voice is (or even if you have one–which, I assure you, you do), you will certainly be able to identify others'. My guess is that you can identify others' voices so well that you could pick out who delivered which lines if you were to read a transcript of a fight among your sorority sisters. Or imagine reading a transcript of your family's Thanksgiving Dinner–couldn't you tell Dad's voice from Uncle Max's? Grandma's from Li'l Petey's? People have a way of letting their personalities and perceptions infiltrate they way they use words. Sure, a "voice" contains trademark phrases, syntactical peculiarities, and personal intonations, but it reveals so much more; it shows us its owners' perspective on the world.

This fact makes your job in locating your voice twofold. You have to hone your own voice, tame it into doing and expressing exactly what you want it to; and you have to render the voices of others, as well. Unless you plan on writing one and only one work in your career–an autobiographical interior monologue (and, if you're planning on doing this, I urge you to rethink it)–you are going to need to learn to portray other identities. This is a writer's privilege and his curse. It gives you freedom to manufacture any type of persona you choose–but it also requires an accuracy in the rendering. Characters aren't always real (in fact, in fiction they rarely are), but they have to be *realistic*. And this means that you must make your imaginary characters totally believable. They have to have the same thoughts, feelings, motivations, and problems as we all have in the real world. Only these are up to you to construct. So, start paying attention–to yourself and to the others who share your world. Because there's your subject.

As writers, we are chroniclers of the world around us, and this means we have to pay attention to that world. A writer never knows when or where inspiration will hit, so she must always be prepared for it. Be on the watch not just for the big things, but the little, almost imperceptible events that measure out our days. It may be the way someone dials a phone or folds a napkin or pulls out a chair. These tiny elements may very well find inclusion in your writing, so hold on to them. Observe the world at the same time that you're in the world, and you will be rewarded with rich, useful material. After all, what's in literature but the stuff of our daily lives? So stop zoning out on your lunch break or on the bus; just think what you could be missing.

EXERCISES

1. It's easy. Have a conversation. If you're in class, pair up with someone near you; if you're solo, pick up the phone and dial. Talk. It doesn't matter what the subject of your conversation is; it doesn't matter who your interlocutor is. Just talk. After a few minutes, end it.
   - Now, write down exactly what you talked about. Transcribe it. No one ever needs to read this, see this, or hear this, so be as accurate and as specific as you can. The purpose of this is to get you started in the actual act of writing, providing you with ready-made "material." Even if it's boring, inane, or non-sensical, your job here is to log it on paper. Now you have no excuses for not writing; writer's block has been obliterated by the preexisting conversation. But, even more importantly than serving up subject matter, doing this requires that you start training your ear to listen better and absorb better. You will have to get used to putting on paper your version of what has occurred around you, and this is a simple and helpful way to begin doing just that.
   - Here is the trickier part. Ideally, you would not have read this part before embarking on your conversation, but even if you have, it doesn't matter all that much. Think back on your conversation and begin writing about it once more, only this time, write about anything and everything that occurred while you were talking *except* the conversation itself. Omit the dialogue entirely, but write about all the stuff that happened simultaneously. Were you biting your nails? Did you notice a bug? See a beautiful girl? Hear other people's conversations? Any doodling? Gesturing? Thoughts running through your head? Put it all down. Include none of the words you and your interlocutor spoke, but include everything else. Of course, this is the real training. Life is going on all the time, all around us; it is your job to notice it. Don't worry about fashioning it into fine fiction just yet; simply get accustomed to

recognizing the myriad activities that surround us as the potential contributions to our writing that they may become.

2. Choose someone at random. It may be a member of your class; it may be someone eating across the cafeteria from you; it may be your roommate sitting at her desk. Make sure he or she is visible to you as you begin the exercise.

- Without describing any element of his/her appearance–not hair color, clothing, shoe size, or nail polish–render a character sketch. For this to be effective, you will have to rely on particulars such as mannerisms, behaviors, accents, intonations, gestures, and any other personality tics unique to your subject. Does she shrug her shoulders when she talks? Does he sit with his legs lounged out in front of him? Does she deliver every sentence as if it were a question? Write on the desk? Jiggle her legs? Touch you for emphasis? Does he have a signature laugh? Play with her phone? Pay attention to the minute details we often overlook in our observations, and include them in your description. Make a note of any and all of the ways your subject comports him/herself and write them down.

- Read your sketch aloud either to the class or to a friend. Can your audience guess whom it is you're describing? Have you caught in your portrait the essence of your subject? If your audience hasn't observed your subject, but is hearing only your description, make sure that they are able to formulate a realistic visual image of the person you are describing. After you've read your work, if you feel comfortable, feel free to ask for any suggestions from your audience; however, if sharing your work still makes you anxious, hold off inviting comments just yet. There is plenty of time ahead for you to develop your confidence as a writer; but don't lose sight of the fact that an integral element of the creative writing process is learning to share your work with an audience, so do not delay this for too long. This exercise is a true test; not only are you discovering how developed your talent is for capturing a character, but you are taking (or getting ready to take) your work public by sharing it with an audience. You are beginning to open yourself up to the feedback and criticism of others, a necessary undertaking for a writer. You are officially on your way!

CHAPTER TWO:

FOCUSING ON DETAILS

Show me; don't tell me. Have you heard that before? And if so, what does it mean? It means that, as a *creative* writer, your job is not to summarize or condense or report; your job is to describe so thoroughly that I can see it, feel it, and understand it–whatever "it" may be. For this to happen, I need details, and lots of them. Concrete, specific details. Imagine you're on the phone with a friend who went to an amazing party the night before. When you ask her how it was, does a mere "okay" answer your question? Or do you want to know how many people crashed, if the guy you like was there, whether the police had to come, if there were any fights, and how late it lasted? My guess is that, unless you're jealous that she was there and you weren't, you want to know all the specifics. Conversely, imagine a conversation you might have with your boss or professor or grandmother about a party you went to; wouldn't you be kind of vague? Wouldn't you generalize and keep all description superficial and brief? We all know how to obscure, and we all know how to reveal–we just do them at different times in different situations. However, in your writing, you have to train yourself never to obfuscate; instead, always provide the specifics.

One of the worst habits to fall into is becoming lazy about your writing, thereby requiring your audience to do the work of filling in the details you neglected and guessing at what it is you meant to express. You're not creating *Mad Libs*, are you? You're not developing a secret code in some foreign language, right? So, be clear. Give us all the facts we need. Even if you're developing a highly figurative work constructed of symbol and metaphor, you still need the concrete specifics. All semiotics require something real and tangible to attach meaning to. For example, let's say you're inspired to write about a guy sitting across from you on the subway. You could, were you to write about him, say, "He was nervous." Or, better yet, you could construct a metaphor of the fleeting subway that implies his nervousness and blah, blah, blah. Or, best of all, how about this: you put down in however an artful way as you choose the fact that he chewed his upper lip until the raw skin was exposed, jiggled his ankle until his shoe came loose, or bit three of the nails on his left hand until blood pooled in the cuticles. Use them as symbols if you like, but use them. Readers want the message to be clear. Even T.S.Eliot, that most elusive of poets, knew to rely on concretes; he took the rather vague notion of springtime and anchored it with the image of lilacs. Get it? We want to be the friend on the phone, not your boss. We want the details, not the summing up. Show it to us; don't report on it.

EXERCISES

1. Describe someone's hands. This exercise is an easy way to begin (or to perfect) blending the concrete with the symbolic. As you describe the hands, you should be aware of the image you are constructing with each detail that you select. Every detail should contribute to the overall image.
   - Begin by visualizing a person, fictionalized or actual. Have a clear sense of who he/she is. What is his age? What is her job? Married or widowed? Kids? Rich or poor? Well-dressed? Now, begin to ask yourself more difficult questions about this person. Is he honest? Does she like her mother? Do you trust her? Is he fun? In your description of this person's hands, make sure that most of these questions are answered by the details you provide. You are going to have to find a way to describe someone's character through the specific details of a simple hand. This will train you to look closely at all the various elements that comprise our identities, and it will help train you to depict those elements in terms that will be recognizable to your audience.
   - Next, begin by visualizing just the hands. You are looking at the hands of a person you know nothing about. Again, these hands can be purely imaginary or they can be real. If you need, choose the hands of a member of your class with whom you aren't acquainted, or choose the hands of a person at the next table over from you in a restaurant, on the subway, at a mall. Write down in as much detail as possible what you see in that stranger's hands. Afterwards, extrapolate from those details and fill in with a brief character sketch of the person who has emerged through this description. This should help you move back and forth from specific to general, as you draw assumptions about character from the details provided in the sketch.
2. Choose an item of clothing. It may be an actual piece from your own (or someone else's) wardrobe, or it may be a fictional garment. Have the clothing in mind as you begin to write.
   - Describe in as much detail as possible this item of clothing. Do not rely strictly on the sense of sight in your description; include at least one other sensory perception. For example, an old boyfriend of mine used to wear a navy blue nylon track suit that I hated. Every step he took resulted in a swish-swoosh kind of sound which he thought was so unbelievably cool that he would walk in a deliberately knock-kneed kind of

way just to enhance that sound. For you, maybe it's the scent on your grandmother's scarves, or the taste of that ribbon edging around the baby blanket you used to suck on. Whatever it is, in your description, make sure you allow us to see and understand your feelings about the article; this requires that you provide a whole lot of detail in order to communicate effectively with your audience.

Next, make a list of the characteristics and feelings you were trying to convey in your description of the garment. If you are in class, read your description and then your list aloud; if you are working independently, you can either invite a friend to help you, or you can put the list aside for a few hours and return to it afresh after the break. After your description and your list have been read, ask your audience if your description accurately portrays the traits and the emotions you intended. If not, why not? If so, which were the most effective details? Begin to listen to what your audience is telling you; this is the best way to shape your words to your purpose. If you're working solo, you can still provide constructive feedback to yourself by paying attention to anything that you need to either repeat or explain to yourself; any lack of clarity to you will certainly be multiplied for your audience.

CHAPTER THREE:

CONSTRUCTING A SETTING

The setting–where and when your work takes place–is a critical element in writing. It is one of the primary and easiest means by which you can establish the mood, feeling, and tone of your work. Remember back to your first day of high school. How did you feel when your alarm clock rang at 6:45 a.m. on that September morning? Compare that with how you felt at 11:00 at night on the Friday you finally graduated. Very different, right? Doesn't Sunday have an altogether different personality from Saturday? Is May anything like November? And what's the difference between meeting the woman of your dreams at a bar and meeting her at a tea party? Would you prefer a guy who lived at home with his parents or in his own apartment on the upper East side? Want a date at McDonald's or at La Petite Maison? Whether you love a thunderstorm in summer or not, a rainy day in no way resembles a sunny one. All you have to do is pick the background that will successfully activate your characters or speakers in the manner you intend.

Like the clothes we choose to wear in our everyday lives, the details of setting reveal something about our characters. If you're writing poetry, you will need the concretes of setting in order to anchor the emotion you're expressing. Emotions floating in an abstract sea of words will be lost–or worse, uninteresting–to your audience. Provide your readers with a time period (an era, a day of the week, a time of year) and a place (in the garden, on the back seat of his car, on a rocky beach at high tide), and you've provided the framework for emotion. If you're writing fiction, you will need to establish the concretes of setting in order to have your characters functioning in a world we can (and will want to) visualize and understand. Characters in fiction, like emotions in poetry, need to be anchored to something real and concrete; this not only gives us a stage for their actions, it gives us an insight into their motives and personalities. The fact that your wealthy protagonist visits his mother in a nursing home where the paint is peeling off the warped front door in long, wrinkled strips says something about him, doesn't it? Or the fact that the young newlyweds you're writing about have a king-sized bed in the middle of their living room because it wouldn't fit in the tiny bedroom of their apartment. It's just a setting, but it offers so much more than merely time and place. Pay attention to it, and make it serve your purpose; it's a simple means to convey a complicated message.

EXERCISES

1. Describe an unoccupied room. Although there shouldn't be anyone in it, your audience should be able to get a sense of whose room it is after reading/hearing your description of the room's contents.
    - In your description you should include as many details about the room as possible, remembering to fill in all the empty canvases that you can. Take every opportunity to provide specifics about the setting. In other words, do not put posters on the wall without showing us whose pictures are on the posters; do not put shoes under the bed without showing us which kinds of shoes they are; do not leave disc covers strewn all over the floor without telling us which bands they belong to. In your description, all books should have authors; magazines, titles; cosmetics, brands. If there are clothes, name the article and designer. Try to leave nothing unnamed or generalized. This will help you refine your focus on details (see last chapter), as well as establish the base of setting.
    - After you've provided your description, go back and add three new elements to your room that will emphasize a particular reaction or emotion you want your audience to feel. For example, if you want us to feel revolted, add a piece of decaying fruit–a peach, maybe–that has melted its lower half onto the radiator under the window. Or if you want us to think the girl's a dork, line up her My Little Pony collection so they're all facing in the same direction. Try to add something other than visual cues, as well. If you can add a fragrance, a sound, a taste, all the better. Remember that setting should always contribute to our understanding of characters.
2. Describe a job or an occupation by providing an illustration of its place of business. Try to avoid referring by name to the job you're discussing; instead, offer specific details about the location that go beyond superficial or clichéd elements in order to create an image of the profession.
    - Begin by imagining what it must be like to enter your setting at the beginning of a particular workday or shift. If it is early morning, is it light out yet? Early dawn? Middle of the night? 9:00 p.m. on a Friday, when you'd rather be at the party all your friends went to? Monday morning or Friday morning? Get as full a sense as possible of what it must be like to spend a day here, then choose a particular time of day, day of the week, and season in which your writing will take place. Determine the exact time that the work takes place. Even if you don't include these details in the writing, you should have them in mind as you describe the

physical surroundings. Try to convey whatever it is you believe the worker would feel as he spends his days here. What would she notice about the place, having spent so much time here? A stain on the wall in the shape of Bart Simpson? The sound of the furnace that kicks on every day at 9:45? The irritating repetition of an officemate's daily phone call to her boyfriend? That everyone has precisely three personal items (a troll doll, a photo of their family, and a coffee cup that says "World's Best You" on it) decorating their cubicle? Choose the details that are most effective in allowing us to understand the worker's feelings about the job.

- Now, choose three additional elements to add to your description of the setting in order to emphasize a particular reaction or feeling about the place. As always, try to provide more than merely the visual in your description. For example, I once went to a dentist's office and had to sit in a chair that was sticky. The whole time I was reclined, my sweater was attaching itself to whatever it was (blood? Spit? Toothpaste? Sweat?) that had gunked up the back of the seat. So, whether it's an uncomfortable chair or it's freezing because you sit under the air-conditioning vent, provide some detail beyond how the place looks. However, avoid obvious or overused images (clichés) like the sound of the drill at the dentist's or the smell of the cafeteria's mystery meat. Be creative in selecting your details in order to give us a fresh perspective on your setting. As you layer in your elements, you will begin to get more comfortable with the idea of revising your writing and of working in stages or drafts. All writers need to master this skill, so you may as well begin learning it here.

CHAPTER FOUR:

BUILDING CHARACTER

Okay, you've selected the time and place, and you've learned how to show them to us. So now you have to figure out who the players are. Who are the characters in your story? Who is the speaker of your poem? Who is the star of your screenplay? Regardless of whether your characters are fictional or not, it is up to you to provide believable figures to whom we can relate and whom we can understand. In other words, they have to function like real people and sound like actual voices even if they're not. Your players may be good, they may be bad; they may be likeable, they may be repellent; they may be just like you, they may be just like me; but no matter what, they have to have some element of humanity that makes your audience respond to them.

Characters don't have to be real, but they do have to be *realistic*. Remember when you saw *Cars*? I remember when I saw it. I don't believe that cars can talk; I don't believe that cars can fall in love or hold jobs or have random foreign accents. I don't even believe they have faces. But when Lightning McQueen backs up just inches away from the finish line, sacrificing his win in order to help his mentor finish the race, I have to admit to having tears in my eyes. And forget about *E.T.* I cried like a baby when Elliot thought that creepy little alien was almost dead. Yet I believe in alien life forms almost as much as I believe in talking cars. So, what's to account for my reaction? How can I, a grown-up with some sense of how animated films work, manage to get so worked up about a few cartoon motor vehicles or a physically repulsive martian who happens to like drinking beer in the afternoon? Easy. They may be animated, but they act and think and feel *just like real people*. And this is the key. Your characters have to be just like us. Sure, E.T. is gross and ugly and foreign to all of us, but he still wants to phone home, doesn't he? He still loves his best friend, right? And what about the Reece's pieces? Don't we all have to have some candy now and then? He's relatable, and that's the point. Make sure your characters, speakers, narrators, and heroes and heroines are realistic above all else; the rest will follow. We don't have to like them or know them, but we have to relate to them and believe in them.

What makes certain television shows so successful? Their characters. Really, how many new and different medical emergencies or creative crimes occur in real life in any given week? Certainly not as many as prime time would have us believe, that's for sure. So what's with all the hospital and police dramas? Interesting characters, pure and simple. And can't all movies, novels, and plays be summed up by one of the, say, six master plotlines? Yes, they can. So why are there new movies and books and plays coming out all the time? New characters, that's why. If you have characters an audience cares about, the rest becomes secondary. Make your audience care by creating good characters–even when they're bad. A believable, realistic character we can empathize with is a good character, no matter how evil he may be.

EXERCISES

1. Imagine your character/speaker. It doesn't matter if this person is you or another person, real or fictional, human or something else entirely. However, it does matter that you can see this individual as a realistic being with thoughts, perceptions, and behaviors you can understand.
    - Assign this character a habit, and build your writing around this habit. This description should reveal the individual's deeper character, and let us know who he really is underneath his persona. Often, it is through our habits that our truer selves are revealed, so take this opportunity to reveal something about your character that he may not want revealed. Maybe she's a high-powered lawyer who still secretly collects Barbies. Or a playground bully who sleeps with the grimy remains of his satin baby blanket. Perhaps the priest you're describing is so eager for cigarettes that he cuts short a baptism so he can sneak into the confessional and smoke, lighting each new cigarette from the burning ash of the previous one. No matter what the habit, make sure you've chosen it deliberately, as a means by which we can see your character in a new or interesting way.
    - With the same character in mind, write a description of the clothing he/she is wearing. Clothing is one of the easiest ways to show us who a character is, so use this opportunity to illustrate a part of your character. Although in real life we are not supposed to "judge books by their covers," in fiction, this is essential. Evaluating a character's accessories is one of the primary methods by which we make determinations about who this person is. Keep in mind that the details you select will contribute to the image constructed in the minds of your readers, so do this carefully and deliberately. Does he wear pants that are just a tiny bit too tight (which is really gross)? Is she wearing an expensive suit but downtrodden shoes? Is yours a tie-dyed kind of character or more of a crisp button-down type? A heavy-metal concert tee wearer or an Aber-

crombie model? Remember that, in fiction, clothes really do make the man. Select a wardrobe that reflects who this person is and how you want us to think of her.

2. Write about a cell phone conversation of which you only overheard one side. The speaker could be your roommate, a commuter on the subway, a housewife in the grocery store, your boyfriend talking to his mother, anyone you can conjure up well enough to provide a thorough description. As always, your characters may be drawn from real life or pure imagination; however, no matter the source of their origin, they must function and be treated like fictional characters, and, as such, they must adhere to the principles discussed here.

- Without including any of the actual conversation that has been overheard, begin a character sketch of the speaker. Far too often, lazy writers rely on a line of dialogue to transfer information, reducing the writing to a report or a summary rather than a fully rounded, developed moment of *realistic* life. Instead of depicting the shock or sadness a character feels, many lazy writers will simply give a, "*What*? He's dead! Nooooooo!" And then have the speaker sob uncontrollably. Your job here is to ignore dialogue for the moment in order to focus on all the other aspects of communication. What is she doing with her hair that allows you to know she's talking to her boyfriend? How is he gesticulating with his free hand in such a way as to make it perfectly clear that he is angry? What's the tone or volume of her voice? Ever hear someone talking to a new boyfriend late at night? I hope whomever you overheard didn't speak baby talk the way my freshman roommate did, in a voice so tiny and high that small domesticated animals began committing mass suicide. Read the cues your character gives you through his actions, and allow him to teach you about himself.

- After drawing the scene, you can now go back and fill in the portion of the conversation you overheard. The nature or subject of the dialogue does not matter for this exercise; it can be intriguing (a shady-looking guy setting up a meeting spot; a sexy woman describing what she has on; a man in a suit sobbing), or it can be totally mundane (a mother reading her daughter the shopping list; a guy asking to borrow a friend's car; a teen-aged girl discussing the cafeteria's lunch offerings that day). Once, I overheard a colleague at work talking to her husband. It was a brief conversation of absolutely no importance whatsoever; she was simply reminding him to TiVo their favorite show and pick up (and I'll never forget this) two deep-dish Domino's pizzas, one with pepperoni and one with peppers and onions. But she started every sentence with "Now, Mikey, remember to…" and spoke in such an irritatingly condescending tone that I was never able to look her in the eye again, having been witness to the creepy Oedipal intimacy of her married life. I was relieved when she finally quit. What I'm saying here is to pay attention to the sub-text, not so much to the text, of the conversation, because this is where characters live and how they come alive in your writing.

CHAPTER FIVE:

KNOWING YOUR CHARACTER

Unlike real life, in creative writing, you are the only person who knows your characters and speakers. Even if they are based on real people, once they enter the world of your writing, you as the author create and control them. They are *your* products. As such, they belong to you. No matter what happens to them in real life, regardless of whether they are fictional or biographical, they must be formed and manipulated by you as characters. In other words, it is up to you to tame even the most real of your players to become the characters your work demands. In fiction, characters may be imagined into existence in the most convenient or necessary ways; however, even in memoirs, characters have to have a shape and significance that matches their role. And there's only one way to create the kind of characters and speakers you need for your work–and that is to see them, believe in them, and understand them as real, individual people.

Your agents (characters, speakers, "stars,"–all the personalities in your work) must function like real people for your audience to believe in them, and the only way you can accomplish this effectively is if you, too, believe in them. Never think of even the most minor character as a plot device or a diversion or a stock figure or anything less than a full, rounded individual. Ever walk around a mall? Sure, you and your friends are the most important people there, but as you walk, don't certain people stick out? Don't you find yourself wondering about particular people you pass? Don't some seem to have a story attached to their existence? Conversely, don't many of them pass in a blur that you scarcely notice? Don't you find yourself dismissing tens or hundreds of people as insignificant, simply because they don't capture your attention? This doesn't mean they aren't real people; it doesn't mean that they didn't have corn flakes with too much milk this morning or have to see a dentist about that chipped tooth they can't keep their tongue away from. It just means that this is not entertaining or relevant to you. This is the way creative writing works, as well; there are main players who have to hold our interest, but there are many more who wallpaper the background. They're real; they're just not important. However, you still have to get to know them–even the boring ones.

How do you do this? The same way you get to know the guy sitting across from you on your first date or your fraternity brothers or your roommate. You have a conversation with them. You ask them questions. I once had a student who said she thought about her characters so often that she found herself talking to one of them–purely fictional, by the way–during her shower. Now there's a creative writer who knows her characters. Talk to them; get to know them and what they're like. Certainly, you'll unearth (or create) a lot of information about them that will never appear or be disclosed in your writing, but it never hurts to know as much about them as possible, as this is not just the best way, it is the *only* way to portray real personalities.

EXERCISES

1. Imagine your character, speaker, star, or narrator. It doesn't matter if this is the protagonist (leading role) of your work or a minor player. Try to get as full a sense of this individual as possible. Develop a psychological, as well as a physical, portrait of her, without regard to the plot of your story, tone of your poem, or mood of your memoir.
    - Ask this character what he carries in his wallet or what she carries in her handbag, and describe its contents. Write down everything, and allow those contents to tell their own story. Does he have twelve different credit cards but no cash? Does she keep her Kleenex in a little engraved leather holder, or do they float loosely throughout her bag, looking as though they've already been used? What about the infamous condom–does he or doesn't he? Exactly *how* many tampons does she have in there? What kind of key chain and how many keys are on it? What do his business cards look like? My husband carries exactly this in his wallet: one credit card, fifty dollars in cash, his driver's license, and one photograph of the four of us. My grandmother, to this day, still carries a voluminous duffel-bag-sized "pocketbook" containing, among all the detritus, a Chanel lipstick in bubblegum pink that has been twirled into a cone shape because she twists it as she applies it. Will these details make it into a poem or a story? Probably not. But they do help construct an image of these people, don't they?
    - For this next part, simply log your character's responses to the following questions. Do this quickly, without overthinking your answers; ideally, you will know (or be getting to know) your agents well enough that your responses need no lengthy consideration. Refer back to this exercise for as many of your agents as you would like. And feel free to supplement with any additional questions you might like to have answered.

        What is his favorite movie?

What is she wearing right now?
What kind of car does he drive?
What is her favorite television show?
What kind of music does he listen to?
Beer or wine? Martini or cosmopolitan?
Any pets? What are their names?
Favorite color?
Early riser or late sleeper?
Loves Valentine's Day or hates it?
What religion?
Favorite song?
When did he graduate?
Does she like her boss?
What did he have for dinner?
How often does he talk to her mother?
How often does she talk to her friends?
Bonus question: what posters did he hang on his walls as a kid?

2. For this exercise, choose two different individuals from your writing. They may be primary agents or they may be background figures; they may be from the same work, or they may appear in separate works.
    - Which of these characters do you prefer? Which is more compelling? With whom do you identify more? Which is more familiar? Just as there are no two people in real life toward whom we feel the exact same, there should not be two characters in our writing that elicit the exact same feelings from our audience. We should always be able to discern our reactions to any character–even a minor one. This does not mean that we can only respond to characters who are similar to us, but it does mean that characters must be rendered in such a familiar way that we feel as if they're similar to us. Remember *The Sopranos*? How many of us are middle-aged, murdering, Jersey mobsters? How many of us know middle-aged, murdering, Jersey mobsters? And yet how many of us felt as if we knew Tony better than we know our own neighbors, friends, or even parents? He was a character so well-drawn and understood by his writers that everyone who watched was immediately part of his world. Choose any two of your characters or speakers, and you should be able to discern the nuances of your feelings toward each. If you can't, try getting to know them better the next time you write.
    - Answer the following questions about the two individuals you've chosen; you will be forming a comparison in order to develop a more complete knowledge of each one.
        Who is taller?
        Who is smarter? How is that clear?
        Who is happier?

> Which would make a better friend?
> Who would be more fun on a Saturday night?
> Which one would be more likely to get dumped?
> Who would be kinder during a break-up?
> Who dresses better and how?
> Which would you rather have your son or daughter date?
> Which would you rather date?
> Who has the better job?
> Who's more likely to get arrested? For what?
> To whom would you be more likely to lend money?
> Who is a better parent or daughter/son?

Talk to your characters and let them tell you about themselves. Introductions may not be necessary, but in order for a relationship to grow, we need to know who they are and what they're about. This is what writers do, after all: they create relationships between characters and readers. So, think about your characters when you're not writing, and imagine them in whatever situations you happen into in your daily life. It is through this kind of regular interaction that they will become as familiar to you as real friends.

CHAPTER SIX:

CREATING CONFLICT

What's going on here? That is the question we have to ask next. You have created awesome characters and speakers, but you're not finished yet! You now have to have them *do* stuff. Although character is critical (people tend to read in order to find out more about others), no one wants to read just a character sketch. This isn't a police blotter; we're not detaining suspects. Characters and speakers may be the most significant element of creative writing, but there has to be some action. They have to act and have things happen and get into or out of trouble; they have to feel and have a reason to feel; they have to be involved or regret not being involved with the life around them. In other words, there has to be some tension, some problem, some conflict in the work.

Creative writing is distinctive in this way: it requires a shape or an "arrangement of incidents," as Aristotle defined it. Unlike your five-year-old nephew's description of his first day of kindergarten, or the article in Sunday's *Gazette*, or the instruction manual for your new TiVo, creative writing relies on the structures of plot and conflict to make it work. Facts do not matter to creative writing; in fact, they can often lead an audience further from the truth that's being revealed. What does matter is that you provide and choreograph events to activate and motivate your figures. And this is true for all genres of creative writing; poetry, as well as fiction, drama, and memoir, all need to have some sort of action or "imitation of action" (another of Aristotle's definitions) in order to function as such.

Even the most banal romantic comedy or the lamest television show understands that there must be conflict. Could there be anything worse than sitting through a two-hour movie only to discover at the end that boy met girl, boy won girl, and then boy lived happily ever after with girl? Come on! Fairy tales have more spice than that, and we read those to babies. Everyone wants to see a problem develop and get addressed. It may not always get solved (remember *Usual Suspects*? Plath's *The Bell Jar* or "Daddy"? How about "To an Athlete Dying

Young" or *Terms of Endearment*?), but it has to be present. And that is your job, as the architect of your writing. You must create the action, and that action must be built on the tensions of human interaction. If you're a fiction writer, your task is to build your characters around their conflicts (either with themselves or with other forces in their world); if you're a poet, your task is to establish a balance between mood and conflict (too many contemporary poets simply lay bare the conflict with no attempt to address or resolve it). Exactly what the conflict is isn't really relevant, as long as it exists. Just remember that, as a writer, you must construct a conflict and then have the agents react to it–not to fix it necessarily, but to evolve somehow from it.

EXERCISES

1. Consider your agent. It may be the character or speaker you wrote about in the previous exercises (see Chapter 5), or it may be a new individual; either way, you should have answered the questions from the previous chapter about him before beginning your piece. Have the full, rounded image of your agent in mind as you write.
   - Describe a scene or a moment in which your agent (character, speaker, narrator, star) runs into an old acquaintance. This may be an old girlfriend, a long-lost best friend, a forgotten one-night stand–anyone at all who has had some connection with your character in the past. Who is this person? How does your agent behave? What does she say? What is he thinking? Is it a long encounter? Is there a big build-up with little actual contact? Or does the chance meeting lead your agent to hope to rekindle the relationship in the future? Although this may be a brief description, the exercise enables you to consider the various tensions required of poetry and fiction as you move the individuals through the moment. Ultimately, there are only two choices: they renew their relationship or they don't. However, the manner in which they make that choice, combined with who these individuals are, is where the plot, the conflict, and the interest lie.
   - After you've considered the encounter described above, even if you haven't written it out yet, imagine the moment that follows. Briefly write about this secondary moment–the one that occurs *after* the encounter. Instead of describing the run-in itself, you will now be describing the aftermath of the run-in. How has your primary character/speaker been affected? Will this change his mood, his day, his life? Will she pretend it never happened and bury her feelings? How will he respond to this piece of his past, and how does it shape his perspective on the future? We all fantasize about the moment when we will stumble into the old lover who dumped us and broke our heart; in our minds, we are wearing a great pair of new jeans and an expensive haircut, whereas he's gained fifty-five pounds, lost his hair, and stopped shaving. In reality, does it ever really happen this way? Not often enough, certainly. So use

this opportunity to sculpt or choreograph the events as you want them to transpire. This is a different way of approaching conflict; it allows you to follow the repercussions of a former act or set of actions without having to portray the entire back story. This exercise requires that you strip away plot in a sense, in order to focus on the tensions that lie beneath.

2. Describe a scene or a moment in which your agent gets either rewarded or punished for *something he did not do*. Consider what the act is, and make sure you know and understand your character enough to render an accurate portrayal.

- The conflict is clear: injustice abounds. You now have to determine if your character is going to be in the right or in the wrong. Keep in mind that, although it is tempting to write from the voice or perspective of a good guy whom your audience loves, it is often the bad guys who hold our interest with a more tenacious grip. Al Capone was way more exciting than Elliot Ness; Iago more than Othello; Satan more than God Himself, if you read Milton. So, first choose your actor; then you must inform your audience of what the act (or the supposed act) is. Did your guy steal from the collection plate? Did she kick her neighbor's barking dog while wearing cowboy boots? Did he get blamed for grabbing a little girl, when he was actually saving her from the edge of a dock? Did he publish in his own name memoirs he found in a diary on the subway? Did he win the lottery with the ticket he swapped for his grandmother's? This is a case of an unjust or unjustified action playing out for the audience; elaborate on the details to illustrate the moment.

- After you've either written or considered the above scenario, describe what follows. How does your agent respond? Does he break down and confess? Does he let someone else take the fall? Does he explain that he was in the right? Does he keep quiet in order to protect someone? Does he willingly take the fall for someone else? Consider all the options and reactions to the scenario you've established. Each provides a certain amount of tension, and each presents its own conflict. Keep your audience involved and interested by allowing them to wonder how the events will unfold. No matter how it gets resolved or addressed, your audience will be right there with you.

CHAPTER SEVEN:

SPEAKING THE TRUTH

As if finding your own voice weren't difficult enough, now you have to expand the repertoire. Regardless of your genre, you will need to channel voices that are beyond simply your own. In fiction, drama, and screenplays, you have to activate multiple characters, each with an individual enough voice to identify the individual. In poetry, you have to create a speaker appropriate to each poem you write; this means that you must approach every piece with a fresh perspective and offer a new "voice" to deliver the insights. Even the writers of memoirs have to become adept at the rendering of others, as no one (at least no one writing memoirs) lives in pure isolation. Writers must be able to offer fully developed personas as demonstrated in their agents' "voices." Hamlet doesn't speak like Macbeth; Monica sounded nothing like Rachel; the speaker of "The Road Not Taken" is different from that of "Mending Wall." It has to be this way, or the only writing we'd be reading would be autobiography; instead, we have authors and poets capable of creating and offering us many varied voices. Tolstoy was so adept at this that he could move fluidly among all the characters he'd created in his voluminous novels–including historical figures, children, and even, on occasion, domesticated animals–articulating the thoughts of each in his/her own voice.

How is this possible? How can one person become the varied voices of so many? There is no trick or game here; it simply requires a patient ear and lots of listening. Practice is what it takes. Think back to a fight you've had with someone recently. Chances are, the more angry you got, the less you heard. When we're fighting, we are looking to win; we're not looking to understand the other guy's perspective, hear what he has to say, or listen to his logic. You The Fighter simply want him to admit defeat and shut up. However, this is the absolute opposite of what You The Writer must do when you're writing. In order for your writing to evolve and become great, you must put aside judgments, stereotypes, and prejudices; you must be willing to accept people the way they really are. You have to be tolerant of humanity as it exists, and you have to portray it as it exists. This does not mean you all of a sudden have to become a flower-child, hugging strangers in the street and dispensing kittens and lollipops to children; it simply means that *in and for your writing*, you must be willing to accept and represent all the dimensions of real people–even the ones you least like.

By giving them their own voice, you are best able to do this. These are, after all, the words they themselves are choosing to utter. Maybe their words reveal something about themselves, or maybe they conceal, but either way, their words say something about the speaker. Whether through dialogue (most common in fiction and drama) or monologue (more common in poetry), having the figures speak is the most direct means of accessing character. In addition, it provides definition; for, like fingerprints, no two people speak the same way (see Chapter One, above). Your job is to allow the speakers to share their voices with us. This is how we get to know people in real life, isn't it? So, shouldn't it be how we get to know the people we're writing about?

EXERCISES

1. In this exercise, you will be working on developing an ear for the rhythm and patterns of others' speech. The content of what is said is irrelevant for this exercise; rather, we are focusing on *how people actually talk in real life*.
   - You have been listening to people's speech since you were born, so you should have a pretty clear understanding of how they do it. If you think you need some refreshing, go to a mall, your cafeteria, the library, any public place, and sit for a while just listening to other people talking. Now choose a random public event (real or fictional) to write about. It could be a celebrity sighting at a store opening, a fight outside a bar, a crashed taxi on a city street, a dog crossing a highway–it doesn't matter what the event is or how mundane it may be. For each of the following characters, write a few sentences of dialogue in which they respond to the event. You should have in mind who is doing the speaking, making sure to a) keep voices individuated enough to distinguish one speaker from the next, and b) provide some window into their perspective and personality.

     An eleven-year-old boy
     An old man with a hearing aid and walker
     A new mother with a baby in a stroller
     An obese middle-aged woman holding a doughnut
     A thirty-something man in a suit with a briefcase and Blackberry
     A high school girl walking with two girlfriends
     A college-aged white guy with dreads

> A Paris Hilton lookalike carrying a tiny dog in a Louis Vuitton bag
>
> A doctor in scrubs

- After you've completed (or at least considered) the above exercise, go back and describe the speech patterns of several of these speakers. In this case, you won't be repeating the words they've uttered, you'll be focusing instead on the *delivery* of those words. In other words, you should concentrate on the *sound* of the voices. Although we think of this as being important only in drama and screenplay writing (where virtually everything written is a line to be delivered orally to the audience), it is nevertheless an integral part of fiction and poetry as well; nothing rounds out a character or a persona as well as being able to "hear" and identify his voice on the written page. Voices, like faces, are highly individualized; render those of your characters so that we get an even better sense of who they really are. Perhaps your speaker pronounces every sentence as if it were a question. Or maybe he has a heavy Brooklyn accent–or a Boston accent. Does she lisp? Stutter? Does he struggle to use long words correctly but end up misfiring? Or does she speak in short, clipped bursts? I once had a male student who offered me this valuable insight: he told me that guys never swear occasionally. There are swearing guys, and these guys swear *all* the time; and there are non-swearing guys, and these guys virtually never swear. But, according to my student, no guy swears just sometimes. Whether this is true or not, I have no idea, but it's a rule I've lived by as an author because it seems so sensible and accurate. You, too, now have to figure out what cues and tics your speaker has that allow us to identify him, and you have to describe them in your work. This will force you to consider voice and dialogue as a means by which character, as well as plot, can be developed.

2. Create a scene in which two individuals have an argument. You may write their disagreement as straight dialogue, or you may choose to describe the fight through the filter of one of the agents' perspectives, in monologue form.
   - First, decide who's fighting. A mother and daughter? Cashier and customer? Boyfriend and girlfriend? Then draw the argument through their words. Are your speakers calm and rational, taking turns in a civilized manner (unlikely, but possible)? Or are they madly interrupting each other to make their point? Are their voices raised? Is anyone swearing? What they're fighting over is, for the sake of this exercise, irrelevant; what you want to do is master the art of rendering realistic and individualized voices that reflect the speakers. For example, I once got into a fight with my husband in the dairy aisle of the local A&P over whether to buy skim milk or 2%, and before I knew it, I was shouting over him that his sister never sent our son a birthday present. What

birthday presents had to do with skim milk I couldn't tell you; I just know that fights are often not linear or logical or polite. Be realistic as you write out the material of your fight, keeping in mind that this is not a pleasant or formal conversation you are rendering, but an emotionally charged, tension-filled interchange.

- Consider the same disagreement as above, only for this exercise, use body language–not speech–to portray it. Show us how the characters are behaving rather than what they're saying. Body language–as you have, no doubt, well observed in real life–is an extremely effective form of communication. It may even more honestly convey what we're thinking and feeling than do our words. We've heard of the "tell" (glancing to the left, licking the lips, looking away, fidgeting with fingers) that every poker player and liar has, right? Your characters are no different. It's your job to disclose all of the various "tells" that indicate what your characters and speakers are feeling. Does your speaker run his hands through his hair when he's mad? Maybe she twists a ring on her left middle finger when she's thinking. Or he rubs his palms down the thighs of his pants when he's in trouble. I once knew a guy in high school who used to pitch an invisible ball and then pretend to swing at it with an air-bat during every conversation I ever had with him. I have no idea why he did this; he wasn't even on the baseball team. But, whatever the reason, he did it so often it became something of a trademark for him. Find your characters' trademarks, and put them down in your writing.

CHAPTER EIGHT:

MOTIVATING THE AGENTS

What makes people do what they do? Are we all motivated by the same forces, or is each of us acting and reacting individually? Does the same event affect everyone the same way? Are people essentially predictable, or are we capable of surprising even ourselves? In other words, how do humans function? As even the greatest psychologists and philosophers haven't yet figured this out, we can safely assert that the answers to these questions are, for now, a mystery. However, in the world of creative writing that you are constructing, these questions must be answered. In the real world, this may not be the case, but in fiction, poetry, and even memoirs, people's behaviors and responses must be understandable. Even when they change–and people do change–there has to be a pattern, a reason, and a plan for the change.

All of us have some internal drama; we are filled with conflicting emotions, doubts (about ourselves or our world), unpleasant memories or occurrences, fear, insecurity, and on and on. But how does this internal drama play out in our daily lives? People may do some crazy stuff–you just have to pick up a newspaper to see that–but *why* they do it is the territory of creative writing. We're not reporting crime or writing news blurbs; we're composing the score for human behavior. Creative writers take the facts of psychology, history, sociology, or science and impose an order and a meaning on them that they too often lack in real life. Creative writers, in other words, make sense out of the mess that is humanity. And we do this by seeking characters' and speakers' motivations.

In my second grade class, David Fox (aptly named) went around kissing the girls on the playground in order to tease them. One day after recess, when we were all back in class, watching a movie about the solar system, I got up from my desk, crossed the room to where David sat, and planted a kiss squarely on his left cheek. I remember doing it, regretting it immediately, and getting in trouble for it; however, I cannot for the life of me remember *why* I did it. Was it to give him a taste of his own medicine? Was it to indicate that I was above the kissing game? Was it to show him that I liked him? I do not know. And, because it's real life, I'm allowed not to know or remember. In creative writing though– no such allowances are to be made. Your audience wants to know, needs to know, and deserves to know why your agents are making the choices they're making. And you have to inform them. What the reason is is entirely up to you, the writer, but there has to be a reason. Knowing your character will help you identify the reason he behaves as he does, but make sure you have figured out exactly what prompts your agent to do the things he does before you begin writing. Have that knowledge with you as you write *even if you're not disclosing it*; that way your audience will understand the motivation for all his actions.

EXERCISES

1. Choose an agent: a character if you're writing fiction; a speaker if you're writing poetry; or a narrator if you're writing memoirs (yes, even memoirs must adhere to the conventions of creative writing). Plot out a scenario in which your character/speaker/narrator suddenly dumps his or her beloved.
    - Set up the scene and describe the moment of the break-up. Remember that this seems to come without any warning to the beloved; it is wholly unexpected by him or her. Without offering your audience any concrete explanation for why your agent chose to break his beloved's heart, try to convey the reason. Did he discover her infidelity? Did her parents tell her to leave him? Is he in trouble with the law? Is she doing it to protect him? Know why he makes the choice to dump her (or her, him), but do not expressly reveal it. Instead, suggest the reason through means other than speech (i.e., through body language, setting, or spontaneous reactions like tears or giggles). The manner in which your agent delivers the painful announcement should go far in revealing what, exactly, his (or her) motivation actually is, without actually explaining it.
    - Set up the same scene with the same people, only this time, attribute an entirely different motive to the break-up. The agents will remain, but the motive will have changed. How does this alter the shape and pattern of the moment? Your writing should allow you (and your audience) to see how people can be changed by circumstance. In a sense, character is determined by the forces that motivate us. A man who jumps in front of a bus to save a three-year-old girl seems like a hero because we assume he acted selflessly in order to protect her. But if we discover that he really just wanted to get clipped by a public vehicle in order to sue the city–and, in fact, never even noticed the little girl–it changes the way we perceive him. The action is the same either way, but the two stories are vastly different. This exercise should illustrate the significance of motive in apprehending character.
2. You may choose to activate your agents in nearly limitless ways–after all, people can be really weird, can't they?–but the one rule you, as a writer,

must follow in choreographing your agents' actions is that they can never act in random or unexplained ways. In real life, people seem to do this all the time, but remember: *you're not writing real life*. You're creating an illusion of real life that is artfully constructed to possess some meaning and shed some insight.

- With this in mind, construct a scene in which your agent plans to do one thing, but ends up doing something else. For example, a young guy saves up three months of his salary to buy his girlfriend the engagement ring of her dreams; however, just as he's about to lay down the wad of cash on the glass counter, he thinks of something (but what?) that changes his mind, and he walks out with the money still in his wallet. Or what about a rich old man who plans to leave his fortune to his only son, who's a middle-school science teacher in Iowa with three kids and a wife; but right before he dies, the old man's will is altered, naming a woman his son has never even heard of as the sole heir. Feel free to draw from your own personal experience, or come up with a purely fictional scenario. Either way, you must remember to assign and understand a motive to your character's actions *even if this is not revealed to your readers*; this will give their actions consistency and plausibility.
- What if your agent chooses not to change his mind? What if what actually motivates your agent is his desire to remain unchanged? Create a scene in which your agent plans to do one thing and then, in spite of forces urging him to change his course, ends up doing exactly what he had planned all along. Although it seems simple, this is a more difficult scenario to plot out. You will need to figure why he is unable or unwilling to change his mind, but you will also need to create the conflict and tension (see Chapter 6) that activates that scenario and the agent(s). Characters and speakers, like real people, make choices: they can change or remain the same; they can be surprising or consistent; they can make us proud or ashamed. However, the one thing they cannot do is bore us. If your character, speaker, or narrator bores your audience, you have lost them. Readers can forgive a lot in creative writing–murder, deception, cruelty–but they can't forgive boring. The surest way to avoid this, even when your agents operate in seemingly predictable ways, is to provide them with an underlying motive as to why they are not taking risks, changing, or shocking us with any new actions. Imagine a man, married to a cruel and overbearing wife who doesn't love him; after struggling to please her for twenty-five years, he finds himself falling in love with another woman. He decides to tell his wife, so he can leave and begin a new life with his new love; but, as he starts to utter the words, he can't. He decides he has to stay with his wife. But why? Why won't he leave her? His story, ostensibly, is boring: a married man stays married. Big deal. There's no excitement or surprise there, right? But it is in his reactions and responses to his daily life that the interest lies: why does he do what he does? Is it through fear?

Guilt? Kindness? Obligation? Laziness? And this is for you, as the writer, to answer. Even if this is not explicit in the writing, you must know the answer and be able to convey it subtly to your readers.

CHAPTER NINE:

FINDING YOUR POINT OF VIEW

Who is delivering your words? Who is your narrator? Whether you are writing fiction, poetry, screenplays, or memoirs, you need to determine whose perspective you are going to be offering you audience. In fiction, you have the choice of writing in the first-, third-, or, even occasionally, the second-person point of view. In other words, stories can be told by an "I" who participates in the stuff he's telling us about (first-person), or they can be told by an unidentified, unknown, uninvolved voice (third-person). Rarely, authors choose a second-person narrator to tell their story (Jay McInerney's *Bright Lights, Big City* is an example of this), but this remains an obscure method. Poetry, however, is typically delivered by a first-person speaker with such intimate knowledge of the moment and emotion being described that readers often confuse speaker with poet (although this is not, we must remind ourselves, the case); but poetry, like fiction, can draw on the voices of "characters" (Robert Browning does this in his dramatic monologues), or it can offer a more general or universal voice. Screenplays, though crafted in lines to be delivered by individual speakers, often identify with or favor the perspective of one character over another; typically, the protagonist (the star) is afforded more opportunity to display or contemplate his emotions. The result is that we tend to identify with him because we know more about him. And memoirs, though strictly delivered (by definition) through the perspective of the narrator, still provide enough of others' points of view to allow for some element of objectivity in the audience's apprehension.

So, how do you choose which framework you'll use? If you're lucky, the answer will form organically as you consider the shape and form your writing will take. So, as you begin thinking about your story, the very way in which you conceive of it has already unwittingly, unconsciously, developed its own point of view. You may have already started imaging the "I" who's telling your story, or the psychology of the speaker of your poem. But what if you're not lucky, and you haven't yet conceived of the narrative structure? Then, you have to make a deliberate decision. Will your work be benefited by focusing on only one person's point of view, or will you need to be able to provide the insights and actions of others in order to balance the story? The voice of your work is as essential as the stuff that happens in it; you wouldn't consider sitting down to write a piece without knowing, generally, what you were going to write, and you can't start writing without knowing the point of view of the piece.

Imagine your piece is going to be about a plane ride. If it is told by the pilot, we will get one story; if it's told by a passenger, we'll get another. But what if it's told by someone on the ground? What if that someone has never seen a plane–or anything bigger than a parrot–in the sky before? The "story" changes remarkably depending on who's telling it, right? Your audience will always relate best to the person whose voice they hear most often and earliest, so choose your speaker carefully. And, if you need to switch–offering the pilot's, passenger's, and bystander's points of view–then choose an omniscient narrator who is capable of moving among the various perspectives at play. There is no right way to choose of point of view, and you will want to experiment over time with various speakers and narrative perspectives, but make sure that you are aware of the choices to be made and make them mindfully. The point of view is, after all, a guide, leading us through the work; none of us wants to get lost in the desert.

EXERCISES

1. The only way to discover which point of view works best for you and your writing is to experiment with using each of them. For this exercise, remember back to your childhood, and select a kid you used to know. Although this exercise will be easier if you draw from autobiographical experience, you can certainly create a fictional moment if you prefer. The kid you choose can be an old best friend, a pre-teen you used to have a crush on, the school bully, or that *one* kid (you know that one kid?) who always used to get picked on ruthlessly by everyone else. Keep his or her image in mind as you write.
    - Writing from your point of view–the first-person point of view–describe a memorable moment you shared with this other kid. You may choose to be a *retrospective* narrator–an older narrator who's looking back at your childhood–or you may choose to write from the perspective of the child you were as the events unfolded. Either way, you will be telling the story of your childhood encounter with this kid. Maybe one afternoon you grew tired of having the fifth graders from the back of the bus shoot spit balls at you, so you fought one of them at the bus stop–and won. Or maybe, after months of following your best friend's older sister around, she finally talked to you. Or maybe you joined in the circle of kids teasing the picked-on kid, but then defended him instead of ridiculing him. This should come from–or sound as if it comes from–your personal experience. This is the easiest way to familiarize

yourself with first-person narration; you've been telling stories about yourself all your life, now you just have to put it on paper.
- The trickier part comes next: write from the point of view of the other kid. Here is where you, the author, must make a jump into someone else's identity. Not only is this is not your voice or perspective, but you must also create a point of view that is significantly different from your first-person point of view (above)–after all, even best friends see things through two different sets of eyes. Imagine what it must have been like for a fifth-grade bully to get punched by a fourth-grader in front of his friends, and offer us that perspective. What was the older sister thinking when she talked to her little brother's friend–was she flirting? Teasing? Bossing? Bored?–and show us her point of view. And what about the picked-on kid? Surely he had some emotional response to being targeted–but what was it? Have him tell us about it. You may choose to adopt a first-person narrator (the bully, the sister, the target) who's telling us about their experiences, or you may choose a third-person narrator who is, although not present in the story, describing the events as they were experienced by this main character (who is not you). Either way, you will be developing your ability to move among different points of view, an essential skill for creative writers of all genres.

2. As a creative writer–depending on the genre you're employing, the speaker you're activating, and the conflict you're developing–you will probably use different narrative points of view in your various works. The following exercises allow you to experiment with diverse voices and points of view in order to determine which works best in which circumstances.
    - Using the first-person point of view (the framework in which the person telling the story is actually participating in–and usually starring in–the action being described), construct a scenario in which the narrator reveals a shameful act he himself committed. The speaker, talking about himself, lets the audience know that he has done this. What the act is is up to you to determine; as is the manner in which the speaker reveals himself. Perhaps the "I" of your work is a nun who has stolen from her parish in order to support a child she secretly bore three years earlier–but how does she come to make her confession to the readers? Is she bragging about her stealth to us? Is she tormented by guilt and desperate to absolve herself? Is she a compulsive talker? Or imagine a child crying pitifully in the front seat of the bus who ultimately offers up the reason for her tears. She was bullied? Did she get a bad grade? Has she wet her pants? In any scenario, the reason for the confession only matters insofar as it must determine the method of the confession; point of view and plot must function in unison here. Your work is twofold: you must create a voice that illustrates and reflects its speaker, but you must also use that voice as a means by which you communicate the

"story" of the writing as well. We want to know what she did, but we also want to discover why, based on how she informs us of it.

- Using the same people and the same scenario, describe the events in third-person. In other words, in this version, the narrator is not a participant in the action being described; she is removed, unknown, and unidentified. Instead of the nun telling us her story, we will have an omniscient voice reporting the events. Instead of the little girl on the bus addressing us directly, we will have a (presumably) objective observer recounting the story. After you have written (or at least contemplated) the differing points of view, consider the following questions.

> How does point of view change the shape the work?
> In what ways are the versions different?
> Were you successful in creating the narrator's voice?
> Which one is better?
> Why is it better?
> Which point of view comes more easily to you?
> Which are you more comfortable adopting?

CHAPTER TEN:

RELYING ON THE UNRELIABLE

Ever have someone tell you her break-up was mutual? They decided, she'll tell you, just to be friends, or to see other people, or to "take a break." But, whatever the reason, didn't you kind of wonder if it actually was mutual? Because, let's be real: how many break-ups really *are* mutual? The answer is not many–*way* far fewer, in fact, than are classified as "mutual," that's for sure. Why is this? Obvious: no one wants to be seen as having been dumped. Breaking up is already bad enough; the added insult of being the one cut loose makes it even worse. So, what do we do? We put a spin on it, so that we can keep our pride and image intact. It's not an outright lie, because we often end up believing it ourselves; but it's not quite the truth either. This spin is a combination of wishful thinking, skewed perception, and intentional deceptiveness. We're getting one person's take on the situation, and it's far from objective reality; rather, it's a wholly subjective response that can't even masquerade as truth.

Enter: the Unreliable Narrator. This is, quite possibly, the most interesting and complex narrative point of view. He provides you with his story and enough facts to illuminate the incidents; however, his presentation is so biased, so mired in his own perspective, that we have to doubt his portrayal. We have to fill in his version of the story with what we construct as a more accurate reality. Edgar Allan Poe employs this kind of narrator in many of his short stories; madmen, criminals, and deviants are often the tellers of his tales. We know we can't believe them, but still we love the stories they offer us. The unreliable narrator demands an active participant as her reader, and this allows the creative writer to form an alliance with her audience.

The difficulty with using this type of narrator is that you, as the writer, have to do two conflicting things simultaneously: you must reveal enough facts to allow your audience to figure out what's really happening *at the very same time* that you're obscuring that reality by the narrator's inaccurate rendering of those events. You have to hide and show at one and the same time. This can be tricky, unless you remember back to our dumped friend from above, or think of other conversations you've had in which people slant the truth in order to portray themselves in a more advantageous manner. "Did you make the team?" you may ask a friend. And his response, "Well, I decided that running around on a field with a bunch of guys in spandex pants touching each other's butts wasn't my scene," lets you know loudly and clearly that he was cut. It takes practice to listen between the lines; people's stories often lie in the gaps of what they tell us.

Hence, unreliable narrators must, while believing that they're concealing the ugly truth, actually reveal it unwittingly. There are numerous ways in which they can do this: they may offer too many excuses, they may provide irrelevant details, they may switch topics of conversation, they may stall for extra time. Simply think of all the times you've understood a particular situation independently of–or even in spite of–the words someone has used to explain it to you. How did you figure it out? You listened, observed, and analyzed, and, ultimately, you were able to determine for yourself what really happened. Now, you must allow your audience to enact the same process with your narrator by having him provide enough facts that the reality can emerge at the same time that his bias and (mis)interpretation of the events are clearly conveyed.

EXERCISES

1. Remember (or imagine) a time when you were cruel to your mother. Although this may be an autobiographical moment, you must treat it like fiction; in other words, even real life, if it becomes a part of your creative writing, must not read like a report of actual events. This is not a transcript; it is an artfully arranged piece. Choose or emphasize details, events, and actions that add tension and interest to your work; your aim is not to relay facts but to engage your audience.
   - As you write your piece, attempt to provide a justification for your actions. You have to convey what you actually did or said to her, but the focus should be on explaining why you felt it was necessary. Once, when my mother wouldn't let me see my boyfriend on two consecutive weekend nights, I wrote, "I hate my mother" in nail polish on the full-length mirror in my closet and left the door wide open so she could see it. At the time, it seemed like the perfect response–it wasn't overly destructive, it didn't require any work to clean it off on her part, it didn't cost anything. I defended my actions by believing that she deserved it. That she was trying to ruin my life. That she had always been opposed to my having fun. That–and this is the worst–because she was unhappy, she wanted me to be unhappy. In fact, I convinced myself that it wasn't nearly large enough a retaliation for her tyranny. Classic unreliable narrator. Now, construct your own.
   - Create a list of possible justifications, excuses, fantasies, explanations, or defenses that could contribute to an unreliable narrator's self-delusion. Think of the many ways and reasons for us to lie to others and

ourselves. Insecurity about how others perceive us; fear that our image will be besmirched or ruined; selfishness in thinking we are more important than others (or than we really are), and the list goes on. Try to be as comprehensive as possible; you never know when you will become inspired to adopt one of these motives for your unreliable narrator's deceptions.

2. Construct an unreliable narrator who speaks about a fight he or she had. As always, even if the events in your writing are autobiographical, you must treat them as if they were fiction, choosing specifics, names, and incidents that will engage your audience.
    - In this scenario, your narrator (and this may be the teller of a prose story, the speaker of a poem, the star of a screenplay, or even the voice during a particular episode in a memoir) has caused a fight with someone she knows. What has she done? She may have cheated with her roommate's boyfriend, broken her curfew, given her boss the finger, borrowed her sister's clothes without asking. Whatever the circumstances and whomever her opponent, the fight should be her fault; she has done something to upset or anger someone else. Now, have her tell us about the fight from her point of view. Make sure to include enough detail that your audience knows what really happened (that she was the one responsible for the fight); however, you must also provide enough of the speaker's psychology to allow us to figure out what she's done, why she's done it, and how she's justifying or dismissing it.
    - After you have written (or at least considered) your piece, make a list of the *facts* of the story. These facts should be stripped of any sort of narrator's interpretation; they should be the bare bones of the "plot" of the work. These facts may (or may not) appear in the text of what you've written, but you should have them in mind and be able to identify them. Your list will depend on your work, but it may include answers to these kinds of questions:
        What is the narrator's relationship to the opponent?
        What is the act that prompted the fight?
        How did the fight begin?
        Who addressed whom first?
        What was the tone of the first comment?
        How did the other respond?
        Did it get physical?
        Who threw the first swing?
        When did the narrator first divert from truth?
        Why then?
        Does he lie, deflect, accuse, justify, or minimize his actions?
        Does the opponent know the truth?
        At what point do we know she knows?

Does the narrator know we don't believe her?
Does the narrator confess or concede?

Answering these questions will help you construct a more comprehensible and believable unreliable narrator.

CHAPTER ELEVEN:

TAKING THE TIME

Surely, you've heard someone tell a story about something that happened two months earlier, but they tell it in present tense, as if it's happening *rightnow*. It always goes something like this:

"So, I'm driving down the highway," the guys begins–often, acting it out with his hand on an invisible steering wheel in front of him. "And this cop comes out of nowhere, pulls me over, and gives me a ticket...." Or however it ends.

This is odd, I recognize–even without the pretend steering wheel. Why tell a story that is clearly *not* happening now as if it were happening now? And yet, I've found myself doing it on occasion; it's a nearly impossible chronology not to slip into sometimes. But why? I think the answer is that narrators and speakers like to create excitement, and by placing their audiences in the very moment of the action, there is a certain tension established. So, inevitably, we will hear people describing dates, recounting fights, or simply summarizing movie plots, in the present tense, even though these speakers are, say, waiting on line at Burger King while they're retelling it months and months after the fact. Odd or not, in everyday dialogue, this is common practice; after all, no one expects us to speak with the forethought required of great literature. However, in creative writing, we need to be much more deliberate in our choice of chronology. Common habits or particular patterns of speech may be forgiven in discourse, but not in writing. What this means is that you must select the time sequence of your piece with careful deliberation.

But what do "chronology" and "time sequence" mean in terms of your writing? Simply put, they are the structures your work employs to convey the movement of time. Present tense, past tense, flashback, retrospective–all of these are devices selected by a writer to communicate time's passage. When a writer uses the present tense, she establishes an immediacy and a tension in her work; what will happen? We don't know, can't know, because even the agents themselves haven't been there yet to find out. If she uses past tense–the method most often employed by writers–she offers consistency, believability and a certain reflectiveness that the present doesn't. If she uses flashback–that fleeting glimpse at a prior moment offered at a critical moment in the present (think of a bride recalling the kiss of her lost first love just as the priest announces, "You may now kiss the bride!" to her new husband)–she juxtaposes past and present in order to illuminate her characters' current emotional state. And if she uses retrospective (see Exercise 1, Chapter 9), she speaks of the past through the filter of the present (*How I Met Your Mother* is a good example of this type of narrative structure, as is *The Wonder Years*, an 80s television show); the events are recounted by an older, presumably wiser speaker. The choice is yours as the writer; but, whichever method you employ to transmit the passing of time in your piece, you must always be consistent. It is confusing and sloppy to slide back and forth between past and present tenses.

EXERCISES

1. This exercise allows you to experiment with the use of past and present tenses in your writing. As you write, keep in mind the need to be consistent within the tense you've selected.
    - Because the preponderance of literature is written in past tense, we have become far more habituated to its use. It is, in a sense, easier to write past tense because we are so accustomed to it. Here, using the past tense, write about someone who found something valuable. What he found is up to you to determine. Love letters in his grandmother's attic? An old man's wallet containing cash from a social security check? An original Picasso hidden under a Jonas Brothers poster? A birth certificate of a sister he never knew existed? What was the object, and, more importantly, what did he do about it? Although you may be tempted to slip into present tense, given the tension of the discovery, resist the urge; the exercise here is to remain consistent in your depiction of time's passage.
    - After you've written in the past tense, experiment with the present tense. Typically, this requires a great deal more concentration, due to our tendency to conceive of stories or poems (and certainly memoirs which, by definition, recount what has already happened) in the past tense. Take the piece you've just written for the above exercise, and recast it in the present tense. Or, if you prefer not to use the above exercise, write two brief passages–one in past tense, and one in present tense–about an embarrassing moment. After you have written each version, consider these questions:
        >Which works better? Why?
        >How does verb tense change the work's dynamics?
        >Which was easier for you to use?
        >Which comes more naturally?

Were you able to use one tense consistently throughout?
Does one seem forced or unnatural in the piece?
Which do you think you will use more in future? Why?

2. This next exercise allows you to experiment with chronological disruption. This is when the work's timeline is distorted or interrupted in order to enhance its meaning. Flashback and retrospective are the two most common types of disruption.
    - Incorporating a moment of flashback in your work, develop a scenario in which someone has been forgiven for a past transgression or wrongdoing. Remember: flashback is the method by which a prior incident or memory reappears to the character for a fleeting–but ultimately significant–moment, and then returns him to his current time, affected somehow by its reappearance. We've all read about or seen examples of flashback–Ricky Bobby reflecting unhappily on his childhood in *Talladega Nights*; Monica, Ross, and Rachel remembering back to their high school era in *Friends*; Othello reminding himself of Desdemona's behavior with Cassio. The bulk of the work will take place at one point in time, but it will briefly jump back to an earlier time for the flashback. In order for the flashback to fit seamlessly into the rest of the piece, try to ensure that it serves a purpose. The flashback should enlighten the character or the audience (or maybe both); inspire him to change the course of his actions; motivate him to alter his behavior; or cause him to make a decision or take an action he otherwise would not have. In other words, the flashback must have an impact on the events and meaning of the story for it to be effective.
    - Slightly more challenging is the use of the retrospective. A retrospective is a looking back; it occurs when a work portrays the events of the past through the perspective of someone who has already experienced them, reflected on them, and learned from them. For this exercise, describe the same scenario as above–forgiveness of a past transgression–only instead of using flashback, use retrospective. Often this is accomplished through a first-person narrator (see Chapter 9) or through the use of a nostalgic speaker in poetry. James Joyce's short story, "Araby" and Edgar Allan Poe's "The Tell-Tale Heart" are classic examples of retrospective, as is Robert Frost's "The Road Not Taken." Even *The Office* is a sort of retrospective, with the commentary often provided by the characters after the incidents being depicted have occurred. But, unlike flashback, retrospective remains in the past. The events and action (the "plot") of the piece have already happened; it is only the voice through which these events are conveyed that moves into the present. In your work, have the older, evolved speaker or narrator telling the story of what happened, allowing us to see how he was altered by the events he's relating and how these incidents affected and shaped him as

he moved into the future. This will give you the sense of how time can be manipulated in literature to serve your purposes as the writer.

CHAPTER TWELVE:

CHOOSING THE WORDS

You've mastered all the elements of a solid foundation for your creative writing; now comes the less tangible, more subtle aspects that adorn your work. And this begins with the words you choose. Diction–the precision and accuracy with which we say what we mean–is what often separates strong writers from lazy writers. For example, it may be perfectly acceptable to write that a man was "big"–there's nothing technically wrong with the word "big," after all. However, is that the best word to convey what you mean–or is "corpulent," "muscular," or "lanky" a better word? What is the difference between, say, someone who's "pudgy" and someone who's "voluptuous"? Would you rather be considered "clever" or "intellectual"? Is your girlfriend "cute" or "hot"? The words we choose make a difference, don't they?

As a writer, it is your job to communicate an idea as accurately as possible to your audience. It is unfair to demand that they figure out what you mean. In conversations, we can rely on our interlocutors (the guys we're talking to) to participate and help us out; we work together to build an understanding. If you're not clear, your interlocutor can say, "Huh?" or "I don't get it?" or "What do you mean?", and we can clarify or add details. In writing, however, this is not the case. You have to be clear the first time your audience reads your work, or they're lost. If you say that a party was "good" to a friend, she may ask you why; if you say the party was "good" to your readers, they may want to ask you what you mean by that, but they can't. So, either they will lose interest and become detached, or they will have to do your job for you, filling in with what they think you mean–and this is often in opposition to what you intended. What if you describe a boss as "not nice"? Your audience may interpret that to mean he makes you work until 6:30 on Friday nights; but what if you really meant that he gets drunk every lunch and then insults the photographs of your kids on your desk while calling you an idiot and cutting off your health insurance. Not exactly the same thing, right?

The words that you, the writer, use matter; they are what you must rely on to create an image, a feeling, a response. So, writers must choose their words with care and knowledge. Writers must be aware that words have not only denotations (their general definition), but connotations (the subtler, nuanced meaning), as well. Paying attention to connotations is what distinguishes a great writer from an okay writer. In creative writing, you're not just communicating facts; you're conveying truth. And words are the only tools you have or need. Words are a writer's best ally; develop a love and respect for them, and both your writing and your audience will benefit.

EXERCISES

1. This exercise will sharpen your skills as a wordsmith. You may rely on the words already in your possession, or you may (should) use a thesaurus to help you expand your vocabulary. As always, the best way to familiarize yourself with words and their usage is to read, read, read. Good writers are virtually always avid readers.
    - Get a list of vague or unhelpful words that You the Writer will try to avoid in your work. Vague words are words that may hint at or suggest an idea, but are not specific or precise enough to convey it accurately; in other words, they are words that require your audience to do your work for you. In conversation, these words may be perfectly acceptable; in writing, these are the words we have to shun. If you can't figure out which words are vague, think back to a time your mom–or better yet, your grandmother –asked you how your weekend was. The crazier the weekend, the more likely you were to describe it to her in vague terms: "good," "fun," "boring," "quiet," "okay," even "interesting" are all words that obscure meaning more than reveal it. We know this instinctually, and hence, they are the exact words we rely on when describing a particularly debauched, insanely fun weekend of partying to our grandmother–to whom we do not want to confess our wild ways. Your boss may ask how the report that you haven't even started is coming along, and you respond in a battery of vague words: "uh, well," "fine," "getting there," or "decent" are all vague. Now, make your own list. And keep this list for future reference, to ensure that you're not slipping into any lazy habits. Here are several to get you started:
        Good
        Interesting
        Fine
        Okay
        Average
        Normal
    - Here is another exercise to help you understand the various connotations that words possess. Choose a number of words at random–verbs usually work well for this, but adjectives and nouns are fine, as well;

and try to keep the words somewhat general. After you've listed several, go back and provide as many synonyms for these words as possible (remember synonyms? Words that have similar but *not quite* the same meaning–it's this "*not quite* the same" that writers are interested in). When you've thought of all the synonyms you can for the word you've selected, consider the different connotations each has, and think of where and how you would use each one. For example, there are about a billion ways to refer to being "drunk." There's tipsy, intoxicated, blasted, loaded, blotto, wasted, buzzed, hammered, dizzy, fuzzy, three sheets to the wind, inebriated, soused–and the list goes on from there. Imagine writing a piece about a fraternity hazing weekend–would you write that the brothers were "tipsy"? Or would you say they were "hammered"? What's the difference? And that difference is the connotation that each word possesses. Form your own list, but here are several suggestions:

> Attractive
> Unattractive
> Throw up
> Woman (or man)
> Money

Each of the words on the above list denotes something, but there are numerous words that would conjure a more specific image (i.e., "hot" and "cute" are both ways of saying "attractive," right? But don't they have different implications?). Keep this list, adding to it when you need practice, so you'll always remember to be precise.

2. This next exercise illustrates the power words have to conjure images, create ideas, and channel thoughts. It forces us to reexamine the role words play in our writing by requiring that we let the concept be dictated by words, rather than the words being dictated by the concept.

- For this exercise, you may pair up if you're working with a class, or you may use a book, newspaper, or any printed text if you're working independently. The upshot is that you will receive (or find) three random words: a verb, a noun, and an adjective. Your partner can select these for you (or an instructor can write up a bunch of them for the students to pick from a hat), or you can drop a finger onto the page in front of you three times, and the words you hit are the words you will use. The more specific and peculiar the words, the better. For example, bayonet, flirt, and translucent. Or chandelier, masticate, and oafish. How about salami, hurl, and wicked? Now, write a piece in which you use all three of your assigned words. Think about them and let them suggest a story or moment to you. Allow the connotations to develop into a concept for your work.

- After you've completed your writing, read your work aloud; or, if you're working solo, find a friend to read to, or wait a day or so and reread to yourself. When you've finished reading, ask the following questions:

> What were my three words?
> How did you make your guess?
> Were they too conspicuous in the piece?
> If so, in what ways (too multi-syllabic? Too unincorporated?)
> How did the overall piece flow?
> Was the piece awkward at all? If so, where and how?

Inevitably, you'll discover that your audience will be unable to identify the three trigger words–and this is exactly what you want! You want the work to be so seamless in its union of words and concepts that it is impossible to separate them. In addition, this is great practice for trying out new words you may not be familiar or comfortable with. Repeat this exercise every so often, even after you've mastered your craft; it always helps to refresh our lexicon.

CHAPTER THIRTEEN:

STRUCTURING SYMBOLS

Symbols are the world's greatest gift to writers. Symbols save us so much time, verbiage, and aggravation it's almost surprising we use any other method of communicating. In fact, symbols are so fundamental to the way we speak, read, and think, that we often don't even recognize them as the abstractions they really are. Symbols–technically, the concrete representations of abstract concepts–are everywhere around us: in song lyrics, churches, figures of speech, birthday cards, clothing, cars, commercials, you name it. You see an image of an apple with a bite out of it, you know it's an iPod; see a cartoon rabbit with stars circling his head, you know he's been hit (probably by an anvil); see a picture of a boy and girl surrounded by a heart, you know they're in love. Why wear a wedding ring? Symbol. Why raise a flag? Symbol. Why hang a cross? Symbol.

So, why all the symbols? Can't we just say it? The answer is: not really. Symbols convey so much more than words are capable of referring to; they communicate a feeling or a concept that words point toward but can't quite hit. Seeing all the cars with American flags stuck into their windows after September 11 expressed so much more than would a sign reading, "I love America, and I want to display the love and pride I feel toward this fine country." The same way driving a car with an upside-down peace sign for a hood ornament says more than, "I am either proud of my success or deeply insecure about not succeeding enough, and so I bought this expensive German car so you would perceive me as a competent, high-status individual." Really, isn't that lame? And what about those yellow rubber bracelets or the pink ribbons folded in a loop? Aren't they symbols too? And isn't it a whole lot easier to just wear a "Livestrong" bracelet or a breast cancer ribbon than to have to declare to every passer-by that you are, in fact, a decent, caring individual who has donated some cash and maybe some time to these hugely worthwhile causes? Without symbols, we'd have so much more explaining to do.

Because we think in terms of symbols, our writing has to depend on symbolic structures, as well. Not only would it be tedious to write (and read!) a work that was purely literal (devoid of all symbol), but it would be nearly impossible. The difficulty for a writer, then, isn't conceiving of symbols or constructing symbols, as we do this nearly instinctually; the difficulty is taming and manipulating symbols to function the way you need them to in your work. For example, if you happen to mention a pack of cigarettes in a high school student's backpack, you have to be aware of what it symbolizes; or if you refer to someone with bleach-blonde hair, you have to know what that symbolizes. Immediately, we think "Trouble!" for the first, and "Bitch!" for the second (unfairness and inaccuracies of these interpretations notwithstanding). If this isn't what you intended, you'll have to change your symbol. Symbols condense so much into so little; a tiny image carries meaning beyond words' capability. Given their power, it makes sense that a writer needs to understand how and when to employ them. Symbols communicate so much so efficiently; they really are the cornerstone of literature.

EXERCISES

1. Society depends on symbols; they are part of what unites us within a common culture. Consider various examples of symbols in contemporary society, and keep them in mind as you begin.
    - First, make a list of as many cultural or literary symbols as you can. If you've read this chapter's explication, you will have already identified some: a flag, a cross, a heart, a product's emblem. Develop your own list, drawing from media, personal experience, literature, music, art, wherever you find symbols. For example, would visitors from a foreign country understand a reference to "the white picket fence"? In America, we take this as a symbol of the perfect suburban family life. We're not really talking about a lawn enclosure at all; we're referring to an idealized concept of attainable familial happiness. As you create your list, keep in mind that symbols must be concrete images–something that can be seen, described, talked about, or contained; do not confuse the symbol with its meaning. A heart is an actual thing (either an internal organ or a symmetrical shape); what it suggests–or symbolizes–is far more difficult to pin down: love. What is love? Where is it? What does it look like? Can you touch it? Hear it? It isn't a concrete thing; it's a concept–and an elusive one at that. Hence, we turn to symbols when conceiving of or referring to it. Your symbols may be obvious (like the heart or the flag), or they may be far more obscure and personalized (created and understood only by you or a small group).
    - After making your list, go back and provide a brief explanation of what each symbolizes to you. Although common symbols may represent similar concepts to different people, they also possess a far more individualized element, as well. In other words, we interpret symbols through our own individual perspective; no two people perceive a symbol to mean the exact same thing. The heart, for example, while we know it represents love, may be perceived as a cruel and odious symbol to someone fresh on the heels of a breakup, but to that person's newly-

From "Huh?" to "Hurray!" 51

wed best friend, it may be a symbol of joy and possibility. The same exact symbol may even change what it means to any one person over time, depending on the circumstances through which it is perceived. The American flag, for example, changed its significance for many of us on September 11. Same flag; different meaning. Review your list and give your interpretation of the symbols you've chosen. If you put "yellow convertible Corvette" on your list, explain to us what that represents to you; it's not necessarily a common cultural symbol, but if it is still a concrete representation of an abstract idea for you, simply tell us what that abstract idea is. And in writing, doesn't a yellow convertible Corvette convey something vastly different from, say, a purple mini-van or a black German sedan? That's because they're not really cars, after all; they're symbols.

2. Now that you know what symbols are and how they function, try incorporating them in your creative writing. Write about a meaningful gift your character or speaker receives. The gift does not have to be a common cultural symbol (it will probably work better if it isn't), but it should symbolize something to the character or speaker on a personal level.

- Begin by deciding what the gift is and why it is meaningful to your character. For example, when I was in third grade, my father gave me a beautifully wrapped present with a huge pink bow for my birthday. I had been asking for–begging for, really–a fancy dress that looked like a little girl's version of a wedding dress, and I was sure that that was what was in this gorgeous box. When I opened it, of course, it wasn't a little girl's wedding dress; it was a softball mitt. I pretended to like it and tried to get excited about it, but I hated that mitt. Every time I looked at it or was forced to use it, all I could think of was that my father wanted me to be someone different. He wanted me to be a tom-boy or an athlete or a sassy, sporty kind of girl instead of the kind of girl who wore fake wedding dresses to, like, the grocery store. I hated it because I hated the fact that I wasn't who my father wanted me to be. Years later, when I was in college, he mailed that mitt to me with a note. The note said that he'd always loved that mitt because it brought us together; that his favorite memories of summer were of us sitting in the backyard talking and drinking Country Time lemonade after throwing the ball back and forth a couple of times. I cried when I read that note. That's a meaningful gift. And in a story, that gift functions like a perfect symbol–offering different meanings to each character, and even changing its meaning for one character as the story develops. Come up with a meaningful gift you can write about, and see how the symbolic structure evolves.

- After you've written (or at least considered) the above exercise, describe the gift from the perspective of the other character or speaker in the exchange. If you've written from the point of view of the recipient, recast the piece from the view of the giver; if you wrote from the giver's point of view, recast from the recipient's perspective. How does the reference change? How does the symbol function in the retelling? Does the object become a more or a less significant element in the second version? By shifting the perspective on the symbol, we are able to see how symbols are essentially unstable, fluidly changing meaning based on who is interpreting their meaning, and when. In the above example, I thought the mitt symbolized one thing, but it turned out to mean something very different to me. For my father, the mitt also functioned as a symbol, but not of his disappointment in me (as I'd suspected), but of his love for me. Play around with symbols in your writing, and practice incorporating them in a variety of ways; they make our writing more sophisticated and more engaging.

CHAPTER FOURTEEN:

MAKING MEANING

Why do we write? Really, what's the point? And, assuming there is a point, why don't we just state that point and be done with it? Why enshroud it in literature? If you've ever sat through a parental lecture after breaking curfew, or a history (or English) lesson delivered by some dork in glasses, then you already know the answer. We tune out what isn't interesting. Even if it's relevant, important, life-saving information, if it doesn't engage us, it amounts to little more than an annoying background hum. But stories are different. People listen to stories; they like stories. Shakespeare knew this, and hence all the dramas of murder and guilt; Jesus knew this, and hence the parables; the Greeks knew it, and hence *The Odyssey*, *Oedipus*, *Medea*. If you want to teach someone something, encrypt it in literature. From time immemorial, people have latched on to stories and poems as the surest means of instructing, explaining, documenting, and preserving human existence.

Put more simply, literature makes a point. Exactly what its particular point is is entirely up to you, the writer, but there is always a reason for why you're communicating this information. Creative writing is decidedly not journal writing—which may have no other point than to explore and vent your personal emotions; creative writing is writing done with the purpose of sharing and exchanging. We write, presumably, because we have something we'd like to say. If you've ever had a ten-page paper you haven't started–due in five hours for a class you've skipped all semester–you will know what it is to write without having anything to say. There's a word for this kind of paper, and it ain't "literature." Creative writing isn't the research paper you have to submit or you'll fail; in fact, it's sort of the opposite. Creative writing is an idea or an emotion that finds its expression through words; it starts with a point and attaches the words afterwards.

When we were younger, we used to hear the word "theme" all the time in relation to what we were reading. Our teachers would ask, after reading "The

Little Red Hen" or "Hansel and Gretel," what the "theme" of the work was. And even though that word, with its slippery definition and elusive application, is messy and imprecise, it does get us to start thinking about what a work *means* to us. The problem with "theme," of course, is that it suggests an objective, almost tangible element of a story that we must identify correctly and grab onto or risk floating out to sea on a tide of shame and confusion. Rather than thinking in terms of "themes," we should be thinking in terms of meaning. What does what we read mean? What does what we write mean? By asking these questions, we are better able to understand that meaning isn't embedded in the work we read (or write); it is something that we construct–largely individually–from the literature with which we're engaged.

As creative writers, it's not our job to create "themes" or to tell our audience what to think or how to respond; it's our job to have something significant that we want to share, and to tell it in a way that invites our audience to figure out what it means *to them*. If you write a poem, you are free to construct an interpretation of its meaning–but so is each and every other person who reads it. And, the better you do your job, the more willing they will be to interact with your poem and to want to make it mean something to them. Their job is not to crack some code you've created or to figure out what it is you meant; their job is to read your writing, and, if so inclined, to become engaged and engrossed enough to think about it, respond to it, and make it mean something to them. For you, this means that you have to manipulate character, events, and details in order to illustrate or express something worthwhile; it's in this manipulation that your work takes on the sheen of literature.

EXERCISES

1. Although this exercise may not be the basis for epic literature, it does allow us to see how meaning is constructed by writers and readers. Begin by thinking of an aphorism, a moral, or an axiom.
    - Without stating or referring to the saying you've selected, create a brief piece that illustrates or embodies your saying. Maybe you've chosen "Out of sight, out of mind;" your assignment is now to compose a work in which that particular phrase is played out. Say, a minister's daughter goes away to college, and without her father's constant scrutiny, she begins to find out who she really is (does she stop believing in God? Begin drinking too much? Enter wet tee-shirt contests?). Or maybe a soldier, sent abroad to defend his country, leaves behind a pregnant wife only to discover that infidelity awaits him (maybe his wife, hungering for attention, cheats with the UPS man; or maybe he finds true love with an Iraqi resistance fighter). This exercise forces us to begin with a message, and to find and shape the words to express it.
    - Once you have completed your piece (or once you've devised a general plot summary that expresses your chosen axiom), read it aloud. If you are working with a class, either pair up and alternate reading your

works, or–even better–take turns sharing your work with the whole class. If you are working independently, read your work to a friend or your writers' group, or, after waiting a few days, reread it to yourself. Ask your audience (or yourself) the following questions:

> What does the work mean?
> What is the point of the piece?
> What aphorism was the basis for the writing?
> How did the audience determine the work's meaning?
> Did readers identify the aphorism that served as the prompt?
> Does it matter if readers selected a different aphorism?
> Is theirs even more appropriate to the work you wrote?

Invariably, your audience will respond with sayings different from your chosen one; and herein is the point of the exercise. Meaning is in the mind of the reader–whoever that reader may be. You the writer can only control what goes on the page; not what goes on in the mind of your audience.

2. In this exercise, write about an unlikely–or, even better, unlikable–hero. In your piece, create a scenario in which this individual does something selfless for the good of a stranger.

- Begin your writing by figuring out who your hero (or, of course, heroine) will be–and exactly why he is unlikable and unlikely to be a hero. Then decide what course he will take. What will he do to help the stranger? How far will he go for this other person? How much will he knowingly or unknowingly suffer for someone he doesn't even know? Remember Quasimodo, the hunchback of Notre Dame? He was, on the surface, as unlikely a hero as any–physically repulsive, reclusive, and short-tempered; but then he lays down his life for the woman he loves. Or what about Silas Marner, the grumpy, old grouch who takes in a child and becomes altogether changed? Peter Parker is a nerdy weakling–he's picked on by his peers and ignored by the girl he loves–but once he becomes Spider-Man, he saves the entire city of New York from an insane number of pumped-up, techno-enhanced psycho-villains. None of these guys is a typical hero, but each takes an action that elevates him to something bigger than himself. In your writing, create an image of a character with enough depth of emotion to startle your readers when he acts in a way that seems at odds with his nature. What he decides to do for the stranger may be a minor, inconsequential act or it may be a grand gesture of epic proportions; it doesn't matter which you choose. The idea is simply to write a piece that explores how human nature is subject to change under certain circumstances.

- After you've completed the piece (or, at least, thought cogently about a potential piece), try to determine what it means to you. Why did you write this piece? (And your answer should not be, "Because that was the assignment. Duh, you were the one who came up with these exercises.") Specifically, why this character or speaker instead of another?

How did you select the course of her action? What does the work mean to you? Once you've considered your response to these questions, share your work with an audience (the whole class, a single classmate, your best friend, your mother, or a stranger at the supermarket). Sharing your work with an audience is critical; if you haven't done this already, don't wait, and do it now. As a creative writer, you are going to have to do this eventually anyway, so you may as well start immediately. After your audience has heard or read the work, ask them what it means *to them*; ask them what they think the point of the work is. Do they have an understanding of the piece? How do they feel toward the hero? As the writer, you should think about the variety of ways that your audience can interpret the events of your work: do they agree with you? If not, does that matter to you? At some point in the future, if you haven't already, you will be sending your work out into public without you; make sure that, when the time comes, you will be satisfied with its reception by your audience. And that means practicing now, so you'll be in shape for it when the time comes.

CHAPTER FIFTEEN:

MASTERING IRONY

Verbal irony, dramatic irony, cosmic irony–what's with all the irony? And what, exactly, is irony? In simplest terms, irony is the gap between what we say or expect, and the real thing itself. Someone says, "Oh, yeah, I love sitting here studying when all my friends are at a club in the city," and we know that's not really what they mean. That's irony. Luke Skywalker, while fighting his archenemy, Darth Vader, nearly to the death, discovers that his foe is actually his father. That's irony. A guy drives a bus for fifty-five years, waiting and saving for his retirement, but the day after he quits, he's hit by–what else?–a bus. That's irony. Irony is the surprise ending, the twist in the plot, the demolition of our expectations. It's what keeps us reading.

Although we all try to predict or anticipate what will happen next (in literature, as well as in life), if we were actually able to accomplish this, we'd be bored to tears, uninterested in the eventual outcome. We like guessing, knowing that we can't be quite sure. It's kind of like the anxiety of a first date; if you knew you were going to fall in love, get married, raise two kids, have a dog named Mutt, and buy a two-bedroom apartment on the lower East side, wouldn't that take away some of the fun? When we go on a first date, we just don't know what is going to happen, and that's what makes it exciting. Same with amusement park rides. Or interviews. Even getting a new haircut. It creates a new unknown. Irony mimics life in this aspect by compelling us to wonder; and, similarly, it enriches the literary experience by piquing our interest and exciting our curiosity.

So, unless your writing is predictable throughout (which we've learned to avoid in the previous chapters), chances are you've already incorporated irony in your work. And, as we studied how to create conflict back in Chapter 6, we know that all good writing has to raise some issues and questions. No one wants to hear or read about a boy and girl who live next door to each other as children, begin dating at fifteen, go to the same college, get engaged, and then get married and live moderately happily ever after. We need some spice, some tension, some conflict. And it is here where irony appears. Good writers make us expect something, hope for something, wait for something–and then switch it up and give us something else. In this case, maybe the guy figures out that he's gay; maybe the girl had a baby she'd given up for adoption before they started dating; maybe they get married but then realize they can't stand each other. Wherever you decide to take us with your work, just make sure we don't know the route in advance. We may be able to predict the ultimate conclusion, but there should be enough twists and turns along the way to prevent our seeing a straight road. Your writing should be like an action movie: we know that the hero of any action movie is going to live at the end, right? In, like, 97% of all action movies, the hero survives a barrage of life-threatening experiences and special effects in order to have that final scene in which he's reunited with his wife/daughter/mother/first-grade school teacher as the explosions fade out behind him. We know it's going to happen, but it's still surprising and ironic exactly how he manages it. Think of your writing as an action movie; the ending doesn't have to be uncharted territory, but the journey has to be surprising.

EXERCISES

1. Imagine a scenario in which your agent (speaker, narrator, character) has a fake or a forgery of something which others believe to be real. Have the players and the phony object in mind as you begin.
   - Write a brief piece in which your agent fools people–either deliberately or unknowingly–into thinking her fake is the real thing. First, who is your agent? What kind of person is she? Answering this will help you figure out whether or not she tricks the others intentionally or accidentally. And what is it she has that's fooling everyone? Maybe the beloved Louis Vuitton handbag her grandmother gave her right before she died turns out to be a knock-off. Or what if men can't help falling in love with your character because of her luscious, flowing hair–but it turns out to be extensions? Better yet: a guy falls for a girl simply because of her perfect figure; she falls for him simply because he's rich. On their wedding night, he discovers that she wears padded bras and girdles, and she discovers that the three-carat engagement ring he gave her is a cubic zirconia. Any way you decide to take this piece will afford your readers some surprises–and these surprises are the basis of irony.
   - Now recast the scenario, so that the outcome is slightly different. Keep the players the same, and keep the phony object the same. However, in your new version, alter the outcome so that the forgery is never disclosed. Your readers will know, but will the owner of the fake know? Or will everyone *except* the owner know? What could be more humiliating than believing your watch to be an authentic Rolex, while every single other person you've shown it to recognizes immediately that Ro-

lex isn't spelled R-o-l-l-e-x, as it is on your watch? Can you imagine a bride borrowing her grandmother's antique pearls for her wedding day, and then replacing them with costume jewels so that she can keep the valuable originals? In your piece, think about the different meanings that may emerge when the outcome is different. Does the work still contain irony? Does changing the outcome change how the irony functions? Does the irony still challenge our expectations? No matter how you resolve or address the events, the course of their unfolding will be fraught with irony. Irony isn't necessarily a function of the conclusion; it's a function of how well a writer convinces us to believe in, expect, or hope for something he has yet to deliver.

2. Consider how weather can function as a device for establishing expectations in your audience. In this exercise, you can manipulate weather in order to create irony in your writing.

   - Make a list of different kinds of weather, being as detailed as necessary to create an image of the environment. For example, avoid general observations like "nice day"; instead, elaborate on the description by stating that it is "mid-morning on a sunny day in the beginning of May, warm enough that little kids took off their jackets to play to the tune of the birds chirping overhead." Or, rather than saying that it was "a rainy day," you may want to clarify with more detail: "an afternoon in late October, already turning dark even though it wasn't even 5:00 yet, with an almost icy rain pelting down on anyone unfortunate enough to be outside in such misery." After you've made your list, go back and explain the image you were trying to create. Maybe in your description of a snowy morning, you wanted us to think of hot chocolate with mini-marshmallows and flannel Strawberry Shortcake pajamas–write that down. Next, read the first part of your list–just the descriptions of weather, without your interpretation–to your class, a partner, a friend, or yourself (after you've waited a few days); did they get the same kind of image and feeling from your weather description that you did? Were you successful in communicating what you intended? If not, you may need to go back and revise or reselect the details you've chosen in order to manipulate the piece more effectively.

   - After you've created your list (or at least thought about what you'd include were you to compile the above list), compose a piece in which you use weather to establish a particular feeling and tone in the work that leads your audience to expect a certain outcome. However, construct the work so that whatever you've led your audience to expect does *not* happen; rather, the opposite occurs. Perhaps you're describing a scene in which a couple sits on a park bench at noon on a brilliant June day. The sun smiles down on them as they huddle together in their private conversation. Birds fly overhead, flowers bloom at their feet, and the smell of new grass is in the air. What do we expect? A typical love story, right? Well then, have the girl suddenly slap the guy across the face, throw her hot coffee on his lap, and storm off. Or on an awful, rainy February morning, banks of dirty snow and icy puddles lining the road, a depressed girl trudges off to work through the miserable slush. Now, instead of continuing in this vein, mix it up and drop in something happy and life-affirming: she gets promoted, she meets the man of her dreams, she wins the lottery. Are you able to create expectations in your audience? And how does using the weather to establish irony help the piece? What does it contribute? Although this may be a simplistic way of incorporating irony, it is certainly effective in helping us understand how irony works and why it is essential for good writing.

CHAPTER SIXTEEN:

ADDRESSING YOUR AUDIENCE

It is, of course, impossible for writers to know exactly who will be reading their work and when; however, it is important for all writers to have a general sense of their community, so that they may communicate more effectively. Literature, unlike, say, text messaging, isn't intended for a single, private recipient; rather, it is an expression that is shared with a much larger group of often quite diverse individuals. The better your writing, the broader the group who will be able to read, understand, and appreciate it. While lesser writers either fade or disappear completely over time, strong writers deliver such a universal message so well that their writing endures; their writing transcends individual experience, and so can reach and move diverse audiences throughout history. Even if you find Shakespeare's language challenging, you have to love a story about an insecure guy who kills his wife because his jealous best friend convinces him that she's cheating on him, right? And yet, do you think that when Shakespeare wrote *Othello* he knew that American college students would be reading it four hundred years later?

Although the safest way to ensure effective communication with a broadly diverse audience that may span hundreds of years would be to write in as bland and general a manner as possible, this is not necessarily the *best* way. We aren't, after all, writing history books, newspaper articles, or biographies. We are writing literature, and, as such, we have to move beyond *bland* and *general* in order to affect our audience; *bland* and *general* simply won't evoke emotion or reaction. So, what do we do? The answer is that we speak authentically. Speaking authentically is the result of having mastered all the previous chapters. You have found your voice, you know your character, you have motivated the agents, and you have charted the work's movement; so, having done all that, you are now able to speak honestly and truthfully. And it is precisely this ability to be honest and truthful that allows you to address your audience effectively.

Does this mean that, in order to be honest and true, you must employ the same voice throughout all your writings? The answer is easy: no. Imagine Bridget Jones telling her story in the same manner as a James Frey narrator–it could never work. Or what about Robert Frost's poems being delivered by a Quentin Tarantino character? Each writer, in each work and through each character, creates a community with her audience based on the plot, the players, the details, and the language of the work. Choose these mindfully, and your audience will follow. Even if it were possible to guess who your audience will be, it would certainly be counter-productive to begin by speculating about its constitution. You have something you want to express, express it in the best way you know how. If you speak authentically, you will have succeeded in communicating with your audience–even if they stumble upon your work hundreds of years in the future.

EXERCISES

1. Choose two different people to whom the speaker or narrator of your work will be talking. These two people should represent two entirely different demographics; for example, the McDonald's cashier and a fraternity brother, or a baby cousin and a therapist, or a longtime crush and a little sister.
   - Give a brief description of the image you'd like each to have of the speaker. In other words, what is the speaker trying to convey about himself as he speaks with this other person? What is the overall controlling idea he'd like his audience to take away from his story? For example, your speaker may want his grandmother to think he's church-going, law-abiding, hard-working, and courteous; meanwhile, he wants his fraternity brothers to think he's fun, reckless, unpredictable, and slightly crazy. After you've determined how your speaker wishes to be perceived by his audience, create a list of ways you as the writer will be able to achieve this. Your list should include:

     > Slang or swear words you would (or wouldn't) incorporate
     > Details you would include in one version but omit from the other Justifications/ explanations that may be necessary for one version
     > References to cultural events, images, or figures
     > References to people in common
     > Quotations from media figures or family members
     > Experiences (shared or not) from the past

     All these kinds of specifics must be chosen deliberately with the interlocutor in mind. Your grandmother wouldn't know who Beyonce was any more than your fraternity president would know what a reference to

Uncle Al's corn pudding meant. We must choose these details wisely and deliberately.

- After you've completed this (or, at least, considered how exactly we alter our patterns of speech for our audiences), have two individual conversations of your own. If you are working in a class, pair up first with someone of your gender, and then pair up with someone of the opposite gender. If you are working independently, pay particular attention to two conversations you have with two different people. It may be your landlord and your boss, your secretary and your girlfriend, or the credit card company and your Aunt Nancy. Once you have ended the conversations, go back and reflect upon how you addressed each. Did you deliberately behave or speak differently? Did you use words, details, or references specifically chosen for your interlocutor? In particular, how did you shape the image you wanted each interlocutor to have of you? Was it easy or difficult to alter your manner of communicating? Reflect with care, as it is through our own practice and experience that our writing takes its shape.

2. Consider the effect language has on our audiences. Clearly, we do not use the same forms of communication with each person we address; we change and adapt what we say based on whom we're speaking or writing to. This exercise will help sharpen our skills at expressing ourselves to different audiences.
    - Like the above exercise, choose two people whom your speaker will be addressing individually. Again, make sure that they represent dramatically different demographics: a grandmother and a best friend, a priest and an older brother, a boyfriend and your mother. In a brief passage, address *one* of the people in your pair. Although the subject of what you write isn't relevant to the point of the exercise, you should choose a topic that is interesting to you and your speaker; for example, you may choose to write about a first date, a fight with a mother, or a particularly embarrassing weekend. In your passage, however, your focus is communicating in the form and manner necessary to convey the image you want your interlocutor to have. Would you tell your grandmother that you drank so much at a party that you vomited into a girl's handbag? Doubtful. Would you use the words "ungentlemanly" or "discourteous" if you were describing the same event to your best friend? Doubtful. And think how different the details you include would be, because, let's face it, we just don't want our grandmothers to see us "like that." As you write to the first half of your pair, keep these kinds of things in mind.
    - Of course, now your assignment is to write about the exact same event you chose for the first part, only you will have your speaker address the other member of the pair. Instead of addressing her grandmother, she is

now addressing her best friend; instead of her priest, her brother; her mother, not her boyfriend. The subject should remain the same; it is simply the audience that has changed. After you've written this, or at least thought about it, consider these questions:

> How are the two passages different?
> Which words are different?
> How is the overall image altered?
> What details have been changed or omitted altogether?
> Which conveys a more vivid image?
> Which do you prefer? Why?
> Have you successfully reached your intended audience?
> Has your character successfully reached his audience?

Our audience shapes our writing in that it is their impression of us that controls what we say and how we say it; it is our desire to reach them and express ourselves to them that steers our writing.

CHAPTER SEVENTEEN:

REVIEWING THE WORK

Did you think this process was going to be easy? Even if you've now become a better writer than J.K. Rowling, Shakespeare, and Larry David all rolled into one, you still have one last hurdle to clear: reviews. These, though they can be tough on your ego (but not necessarily), are actually one of the most helpful tools at a writer's disposal. It is, after all, through reviews that we learn what our strengths and skills are–as well as what our deficiencies or weaknesses are. It's not always fun to hear, but it *is* always informative; and this information can lead us to improve beyond our own expectations. The key is to listen to (or read) reviews with an open, unprejudiced, and unguarded mind. If we receive reviews in a defensive, combative state, we aren't really receiving them at all. And this will only hurt us. Rather, consider reviews as constructive criticism, help sent from another quarter, or an opportunity for further improvement, and those reviews will inspire us to greater achievements.

The greatest difficulty with getting reviewed, however, often proves to have little to do with our feelings on the matter; the greatest difficulty with getting reviewed is often finding reviewers. People–especially the people you specifically ask–don't want to insult or criticize your work. If they're your friends and peers, then they want to support and encourage you in your writing. They are desperate not to hurt your feelings. But this is exactly what an emerging writer needs–an audience who can read her stuff and tell her what's not clear, what's boring, or what's unrealistic. Without that objective response, we might never know that what we're writing is entirely lost on our audience; what we think is a perfectly depicted moment may be nothing more than an incoherent disaster to our readers. We need to hear their thoughts so that we can improve. However, if you ask someone to read and respond to your writings, you will inevitably hear this–and virtually nothing more: "Good. It was good. I liked it." Huh? That tells a writer absolutely nothing.

So, we need to be crafty. We need to figure out ways to get our reviewers' responses in a way that a) makes us comfortable, and b) makes them comfortable. But how? The answer lies in Mrs. Munson's third grade classroom. Mrs. Munson was my teacher, and, like most elementary school teachers, she assigned book reports to each of her students. When, after two or three of these tedious reports, it became painfully obvious to her (and to all of us third-graders, as well) that all anyone was ever going to say was simply, "Good. *Stuart Little* was good. I liked it," she decided to shake it up for us. No longer were we given carte blanche with those oral reports. Oh, no. We had to dispense with the generalities and get "deep" (that was her word). And from that point on, she provided us lists of questions we had to answer in our reports. Not questions like, "Did you like this book?", but questions like, "What external forces motivated Stuart Little to take action?" and "What internal conflict was he attempting to resolve by embarking on the path he chose?" Or something like that, anyway. We may have been in third grade, but we learned–man, did we learn–that "good" and "I liked it" just weren't going to cut it. Learn from Mrs. Munson. Ask your reviewers the most specific questions possible in order to get the precise response you need. This alleviates their well-intended (but ultimately unhelpful) generalities, and it helps reduce (or remove) the indignation you would have felt at perceiving their vague comments as an overall condemnation of your writing.

EXERCISES

1. The following exercises will use the forms included below. One form is a review sheet for poetry; the other, for fiction. You may choose one, or you may use both and adapt the questions to your particular work and genre. Although we are not objective when it comes to reviewing our own work, we need to make sure that our writing is, at the very least, clear and as well-written as possible before enlisting anyone else as a reviewer. In this exercise, you will be acting as your own first critic.
    - Once your work has been written, put it aside for a day or two. Try to come back to the work with a fresh eye. Now, read the work over from beginning to end, without disruption. *You are not editing, revising, or changing the work; you are simply reading your work at this point*! You aren't writing now, you are reviewing. It may be helpful if you do not even have a pencil or keyboard near you as you read. Try and get a general sense of your voice, the tone of the work, and the shape of the work. Did you accomplish what you had intended? Do you think the work is close to completion, or do you think there is a lot of revision (see Chapter 18) that is required? In general, a rereading of our work tends to prove very validating and reassuring, even if there is work still to be done–and this should be the first step you take in the process of reviewing.

- After you've read your work and gotten the overall impression, turn to the forms below. Select the form that most closely addresses the types of questions you need answered about your particular work. Again, read your work over from beginning to end, without interruption, and fill out the review sheet, remembering to be as specific as possible in your responses. Try to treat the work objectively; if you have questions about the work, or feel there are areas that need to be revised or clarified, make a note of this in the review. Now is *not* the time to make any revision; it is the time for straight review. Make sure you include both positive and negative feedback in your response, as each is helpful in its own way. Keep these forms and read them again for future revision (see Chapter 18).
2. The next set of exercises will also use the forms below. Choose the one most appropriate for your work, or adapt them to your genre. The following assignments require an audience to review your work.
    - Find someone with whom you can share your work. This may be intimidating if you haven't yet taken this step, but, as a creative writer, it is necessary; creative writing is done with an audience in mind–it is not journal writing, after all. If you are working in a class, pair up; you can review each other's work. If you are working independently, this is an excellent time to find or start a writers' group (check your local library, as this is a great place to post or find listings). Otherwise, ask a friend or peer to read your work. After your work has been read, discuss the work briefly with your reader. Get her impression of your writing, keeping in mind that people–especially friends and family members–will probably want to keep their comments general, kind, and brief. This can still be helpful however, if you ask particular questions about areas or passages or lines that gave you pause or trouble in their construction.
    - After they've read the work, ask them to use the written review sheet (below) to guide their responses. Writers working in a class or group may have an easier time finding a critic willing to participate, but those working independently shouldn't disregard the forms, as they will certainly benefit them and their writing. The more seriously your reviewer takes the form, and the more detailed his answers, the more helpful it will be to you. Exchanging works with a fellow writer is, perhaps, the best route here, as the reciprocity enables each writer to provide a more candid and thorough review. Once you have received your review back, read it without defensiveness and keep it for future revision (see Chapter 18).

CREATIVE WRITING PEER REVIEW:
SHORT FICTION

Name of Author:
Name of Reviewer (optional):
Title of Work:

1. PLOT

   a. What is the plot of the story?

   b. Is it tired or overdone?

   c. How could the subject be strengthened?

   d. What scene could be added to develop the plot?

   e. Please provide overall comments about the plot structure, including the one element you most admire and the one element you would most like to see revised.

2. CHARACTER

   a. Are the characters believable?

   b. What do you see as the motivation for their actions?

   c. Do they evince realistic emotion in realistic ways?

   d. Is there sufficient dialogue? Is it realistic?

   e. Are the characters' names appropriate? Why (not)?

3. SETTING

   a. What is the setting?

   b. How could the author make the setting clearer?

   c. What specific element could be added to the setting?

   d. How would changing the setting impact the plot?

   e. State the aspect you most/least like about the setting.

4. THEME AND SUB-TEXT

   a. What issues does the fiction raise?

b. Does it treat these issues in an appropriate fashion (i.e., with humor, sensitivity, sympathy, etc.)?

   c. Is there a sub-text? What is it?

   d. How could this author develop a more subtle sub-text?

   e. What is the lesson or the feeling this work leaves you with?

5. LANGUAGE

   a. Is the language of the work sufficiently sophisticated?

   b. Does the author express himself/herself clearly?

   c. Please give an example of the style of writing you most admired in the work.

   d. Please also provide an example of the writing you'd like to see changed.

6. TITLE

   a. What does the title contribute to the work?

   b. How does it impact you as you begin to read?

   c. If work is untitled, provide a suggestion and explain.

7. CONFLICT

   a. What conflicts do the characters face?

   b. How does the author address these conflicts?

   c. Is there another way to deal with theses problems?

   d. Are the problems too over-simplified? Too clichéd?

   e. How could the author intensify the impact and resolution of the conflicts?

8. CONCLUSION

   a. How does the work conclude?

   b. Is this a satisfactory conclusion?

c. How could the author improve the ending?

d. Did the author choose the right moment to conclude?

9. GENERAL COMMENTS

a. Please state the element of the work you most admired. Explain your response.

b. Please state the element you would most like to see changed. Explain your response.

CREATIVE WRITING PEER REVIEW:

POETRY

Name of Author:
Name of Reviewer (optional):
Title of Work:

1. Please comment on the use of figurative language in the poem.

    a. Metaphors

    b. Imagery

    c. Sounds (rhyme, rhythm, assonance, alliteration, etc.)

    d. Form

    e. Conceits (extended metaphors)

    f. Any other type of figurative language (similes, hyperbole, personification, etc.)

2. Please comment on the meaning of the poem.

    a. What does the poem mean to you?

    b. Is the message delivered clearly?

    c. Too clearly? Explain.

    d. How do you interpret this meaning?

    e. Is the meaning suited to the form and style?

3. Please comment on the style of the poem.

    a. How would you characterize this writer's style?

    b. How does it correlate with the message of the poem?

    c. What is your favorite line or image?

    d. Why?

     e. What is the feeling or mood of the work?

4. Please comment on the areas that may require some revision.

     a. What ONE image would you want to see altered–either developed or removed–in this poem?

     b. Explain your answer above.

     c. How would changing form/style/figurative language affect the work?

5. Strengths of this poet.

     a. Single greatest attribute?

     b. Why?

     c. Feeling the poem leaves you with?

     d. Most memorable image or line?

     e. Provide overall/general comments about the writing.

CHAPTER EIGHTEEN:

REVISING YOUR WORK

    Chances are good that, if you've done any writing, you've done some revising. Most us of can't resist the urge to edit and change things around as we go along. We may have been told to "just write it first" and leave the fixing until later, but it often proves impossible. However, by this point in your evolution as a writer, you have probably completed a draft–or maybe several–that you're looking to polish up into a finished version. And this is when revision becomes critical.
    Ideally, the writing process would go something like this: come up with an idea for a piece, write it, review it, revise it, sell it, give your boss the finger as you quit to become a rich and famous writer. In reality, these steps often blend together in the construction of what we ultimately hope is at least a serviceable piece that people will appreciate. But, no matter where you are in the process, and no matter how little you may love the idea of altering your beloved work, revisions are a necessary step. Many poets believe that a poem is never completed, but rather, just put aside. And this speaks to the ubiquity and importance of revision. Many beginning writers share the belief that their writing is best left untouched, that their original scribblings are the best form of their expression, that revision will taint the purity of their intention. This is a notion best cast aside, and cast aside early. Whatever our aversion to change, if we're going to convey what we wish to our audience, we often need to make several attempts. In other words, revision is necessary.
    Does this mean broadscale overhauling for each piece we write? Of course it doesn't. Each piece is different; some will require more revision, and some less. What it does mean is that we have to know what we want to say, and we have to know how we want to say it; after that, the process of revision becomes quite easy. It may include little more than editing for grammatical glitches and spelling errors; or, more likely, it will include some retooling of lines and pas-

sages that simply don't work. This is when your reviews are most helpful; you've probably noted where you felt your piece fell short, and if your fellow reviewer(s) felt similarly, then you know that's an area requiring revision. In short fiction, every line must count; in poetry, every word must bite; in screenplays; every act must move; and in novels, every scene must matter. If there's a moment that doesn't count, bite, move, or matter, fix it. Make it affect your readers.

Revision is a difficult undertaking, no doubt. It's like a mother being forced to point out all the flaws in her adored baby's face. It requires that we rearrange things in a precious work of our own creation. But if you knew that, by getting a haircut for your adored baby, he could be even cuter, wouldn't you do it? If you knew that, by wiping off the encrusted banana from his mouth, people would pay him even more attention, wouldn't you do it? Revision doesn't mean throwing the baby away; it means improving him in manageable, helpful ways. And, for writing, these ways include checking (and potentially fixing): grammar, spelling, word choice and usage, clarity, flow, transitions, development, cohesion, and resolution. Consider the process of revision a necessary treatment rather than a cosmetic embellishment. It's not lipstick on a toddler's mouth; it's Desitin on her diaper rash. Your work, far from being corrupted by the process, will be enriched and improved.

EXERCISES

1. For this exercise, you may use your own first draft, or, if you prefer, you may use an article, advertisement, or passage taken from another work. Of course, it will be more efficient to use your own writing, but choose what you are comfortable with to get started.
   - Select a work to revise; it is preferable to use a work that has already been reviewed, as it will save you some time. With review in mind (and hand), read the piece from beginning to end, using a pencil (or keyboard) to make marks and suggestions as you go along. Note anything you'd like to reconsider, whether it is rule-based or content-based. Mark punctuation, words, lines, or passages that you feel need some attention, but do not attempt to fix all of these as you go through. Rather, on the first pass, focus strictly on the actual errors (in grammar, usage, or spelling), and correct these. If you are unsure of how to make these corrections, highlight them, then refer to a usage handbook–or editorial assistant, if you have one–for help. Errors of this nature are the easiest to fix, as there are clear-cut rules we must follow in our language. These do not (or should not) affect content, so start with this kind of correction.
   - After you've made the appropriate corrections to grammar, usage, and spelling, go back and consider the marks left near lines and passages that need more content-based revision. These may include passages that lack development, lines that aren't coherent, transitions that aren't

smooth, or any detail that needs to be either eliminated or expanded. This kind of revision is more difficult, as it requires more creative sorts of solutions. If at any point what you're reading is unclear–if you find that you are either confused because of too many omissions or assumptions on the author's part, or if you find that you are filling in extra information (particularly when revising our own writing) that isn't in the actual piece, then here is the chance to fix it. Remember that if you are asking questions of the work and not getting answers, then those answers must be included in the revision. We are especially guilty of this when revising our own writing; we want to justify or explain why we chose to include unnecessary information or to omit necessary information. Ultimately though, it is our audience who gets to determine this, because if they want something and it's not there, they won't appreciate our writing. So, even though it's up to you if and how you fix something, it has to serve the needs of the people reading your work. You aren't going to be there to explain to each person who reads your work why you made the decisions you did about your work. So, with them in mind, revise now for clarity and content.

2. One of the most common errors writers make is to rush themselves. You may very well have seen this in your own work (or felt it while composing the work). That is to say, we want to communicate a whole lot of stuff, but we don't want to take too long to do it. This exercise is designed to help us expand our ideas without becoming wordy, boring, or reporterly in our writing.

- Choose a piece of writing to work on, preferably one of your own, and find the line or passage you feel is most rushed. You may not think any are rushed, in which case, find one that you feel could most bear some expansion. Remember that this is only an exercise; you do not have to keep these revisions if you choose not to. Now, as you revise the passage, expand the moment. It may be a passage when we resort to summarizing in order to condense our characters' pasts; it may be a line that we've cut off in order to keep true to the rhythm of the poem; it may be a scene cut out of our script in order to fit into the twenty-two minutes a sit-com has to offer. No matter the genre or reason, expand this section. While there may be limits on word count, page numbers, or show length, there is no limit on how much revision you're allowed to undertake here. Even if it seems to ruin your intention, write out the expansion and follow it through. For example, rather than writing, "Dan and Cat fell in love in high school, went to college together, got married, and now lived in a house near their parents," you may want to stop, pause, and insert a scene that illustrates this without listing it like an obituary. Maybe something like this: "Dan first saw Cat as she walked past the shop class door his sophomore year; he noticed that she carried the same faded red L.L.Bean backpack he did. Only years later, long after they had gone to the prom together, lived in dorms across the hall from each other, and toasted with the silver goblets his mother gave them for their first wedding anniversary, did he remember that he had also noticed that she walked with a sad sort of hunch, as though she expected the world to be cruel to her." Now, find a passage you can embellish with extra details–removing lists, summaries, reports, or abbreviated moments of any kind. Draw a picture; don't give a caption.

- After you've expanded your moment(s), read the revised version to your audience. If you're working in a class or writers' group, pair up and exchange works with a peer; if you're working independently, find a reader to help you, or wait a day or two, then come back with a fresh eye to reread your work. Compare the two versions. Without regard to meter, rhythm, flow, or length, which version offers a fuller image? If your expanded version is preferable to you, you now have to find a way to incorporate the changes–and this may mean cutting out unnecessary information from other scenes or lines. If your original is preferable, you will still need to revise it (even if this means without expanding it); you wouldn't, after all, have chosen this particular part if you didn't have some feelings of ambivalence about its completion. The idea of these exercises in revision is not simply to have you rework your writing with an eye on linear improvement, but rather to get you thinking about and practiced in the art of linguistic manipulation. Writing is malleable, changeable, and adaptable; we can make what we want of it. Ultimately, we hope that we work our piece into better shape than we started with, but even if, in the end, it's neither better nor worse–merely different–that's fine, too. The revisions themselves may even prove to be a launching pad for further writings. So, think of revision as an integral part of the writing process, because, after all, it is.

CHAPTER NINETEEN:

POLISHING YOUR MANUSCRIPT

It may be in a file on your computer; it may be in stacks of looseleaf paper; it may be in bunches of cocktail napkins, business cards, and wrinkled Kleenex, but wherever it is, you now have a working "final" version. Congratulations! You've lived with it, thought about it, and slaved over it. You've muscled it into the shape you want, and it's pretty good. No, it's *really* good. Damn it, it's awesome. Umm, so, now what?

No matter what form it may be in, you now have to create a presentable manuscript–an intimidating concept, no doubt. The very word–*manuscript*–sounds imperious and elusive, doesn't it? But don't let the word fool you, you already have a manuscript–it's the thing you've been working on. A manuscript, quite simply, is the written work before it gets published. It's the "polishing" part of the chapter title that poses the challenge here. And this actually takes some work. If you've been diligent in your reviewing and revising, then your manuscript should be in working order. There should be no grammatical errors, no spelling or usage issues, and no content problems. Unfortunately though, that doesn't mean it's finished. For those writers who compose on the computer, you've cut your workload in half; for those who can only write longhand, now's the time to get typing. The simple fact is that everything you share, send out, or submit needs to be typed. No one reads actual handwriting anymore, so start familiarizing yourself with your keyboard; you'll need it. Rule one of manuscript preparation is type, type, type.

Next, of course, you'll need a title. If you didn't already think of one, change it twenty times, consider seventeen others, then finally come up with the perfect one at the last minute, I suggest you get going now. Titles are like tee-shirt slogans: we've seen a million of them, we just don't remember them all. Let your title be the "I'm With Stupid" or the "My Parents Went to the Bahamas and All I Got Was This Lousy Tee Shirt" slogans we never forget. Choose a title that is descriptive or indicative of the work and its tone, but make sure it has some spice that will capture the attention of an audience (and a market) that has little patience, time, and generosity when it comes to selecting its reading material. So, choose–but choose wisely. And keep in mind that, down the road, your publisher may ask (demand) that you change the title, so never discard your earlier considerations; you just may end up having to call on them at some point.

From here, the rules get a little more fast and loose. If you've written multiple pages, you will paginate the work, providing not just page numbers but a brief header, as well. Often, this is either the title or an abbreviation of the title that accompanies the page number at the top (or, if you prefer, bottom) of the page; although it can also be the author's last name adjoining the page number. Unless you have specific guidelines provided by an agent or editor, choose whichever you prefer. You will also include a cover page that has all the necessary information laid out in an appealing, easy-to-read format. This information includes the title of the work, your name, your affiliation (if relevant), word count (or line count for poetry), and contact information (phone number and email definitely; address is optional). All pages should be pristine–unmarked and unfolded–and printed in a "normal" (read: *not* quirky) 11 or 12 point font. Lines should be double-spaced (or 1.5) and have standard borders and margins. In other words, let your writing speak for itself; do not rely on any visual tricks on the page to sell your work for you.

As you prepare to send out your manuscript, consider including two additional items: a brief author's bio and a brief description of the work. Think of a book jacket and the information contained therein, and use this as your model. Your author bio should be a few significant lines that encapsulate who you are and what you have written (and published) before. Include here any information that may help a potential reader choose you over another writer. Read several author bios to get a sense of the format, and then create one that accurately represents you. For the blurb about the work, you can provide a little more detail, but don't overdo it; this theoretically should fit on the inside flap of a book. Maybe include a significant quotation from the work, followed by a synopsis or overview. Brevity here is key.

Lastly, but perhaps most importantly, before sending your work anywhere, you should copyright it. There are several ways to do this, including a "poor man's copyright" and an official Library of Congress copyright. The "poor man's" version requires that you send yourself a copy of the work through the post office and keep the contents sealed with the postdate in place until such a time as you may need it to prove that the work is, in fact, your original creation. The safer method is to submit the requisite form and payment to the Library of Congress for an official copyright. All necessary information is available online, at the Library of Congress's website. If you plan on distributing or publishing your work (particularly if you intend to do this electronically), you would be well advised to copyright through the Library of Congress. Although there is a charge for this service, it may very well be worth it for the peace of mind (and legal protection) it provides. However you choose to protect the integrity of your creation, be smart: take precautions now to ensure that your position as the original author is never jeopardized.

EXERCISES

1. This exercise will certainly help you as you compile your final materials to submit to agents and publishers. For this assignment, you will be composing your author's bio.
   - In a few brief sentences (not more than a half-dozen or so), convey to your audience the pertinent facts about who you are. Your bio should not be glib or boastful; rather, try for a tone of sincerity and candor. State things as they are, without embellishments. Consider including information such as:
     > Profession (if relevant)
     > Education (if relevant)
     > Other writing you've done
     > Publications
     > Area where you live (not your address)
     > Significant family members
     > Contact information (websites, blogs, or email)
     > Photo

   Certainly, you should mention any distinctions or accomplishments you've achieved, and this includes having had your work printed in local papers or college literary journals; simply state the titles of the publications that have published your material. However, if you are a newly emerging writer, then don't despair at not having much to claim in terms of your experience or publications. Simply focus on who you are and where you came from instead.
   - Now, after you've finished your actual bio, compose one for the writer you would like to be. How does the information change? What awards will be included? What kinds of writing will you have done? And what is your tone? For an emerging writer, the tone should be straightforward; for a renowned writer, the rules become far more flexible. Try to keep consistent with the tone of the work in your fictionalized author bio. If your work is humorous, you can be light; if your work, however, is somber, take a more direct tone in your bio. Keep this bio with you; not only is it good practice for composing these sorts of thing, but it just may serve as the inspiration you need as you move forward in your path as a writer.
2. In this exercise, you will be writing a brief book description to go along with your author bio. You may want to investigate the format of these before getting started; check out your library or bookstore to find out more about the content of these book jacket blurbs.
   - Although your book description will certainly be longer than your author bio, it should still be kept brief and to the point. First, select a quo-

tation, a line, or a very short passage that you would like to include as a sort of epigraph. The quotation should represent what the overall work is about. If you wrote a comical novel, then choose a funny quotation; if you wrote a collection of melancholy odes, then choose a particularly reflective line. Remember, you're ultimately trying to appeal to potential readers (and buyers), so make your decision with them in mind. After your epigraph, begin with an engaging description. We're all familiar with that movie-description guy's voice beginning every commercial for a film with, "In a world where...," and somehow working in that "this time, it's *personal*." Right? Well, consider this your turn to advertise your work. How do you start? What kinds of things do you want to include? And how much of the plot or collection do you want to reveal? You want to tempt and tease you potential readers, but you don't want to bait them with what looks like too obvious of a lure–so avoid the implication that they must buy the book if they want to find out what happens. Make sure the description adequately reflects the work; no one likes being deceived. So, treat your audience with respect and honesty as you prepare your book jacket description, but don't be ashamed to promote it. You are trying to sell it, right?

- After you've written a draft (or two) of your book jacket blurb, share your description with others. If you are working in a class, exchange your descriptions with several of your classmates; if you are working independently, distribute your blurbs to friends, librarians, teachers, or family members. Invite as many people as possible to read your "book jacket," and then get their responses. Because this is merely a description of the work, not the work itself, people tend to be more comfortable offering their honest opinion; and remember that candor in a critic is highly helpful. After all, this brief description is often what attracts or deters a potential reader. Take any and all suggestions seriously, and try to accommodate their points; they are your potential audience, so you should listen to them. You may want to ask them specific questions to guide their critique, such as:

  > Based on this brief description, would you read it?
  > Based on this brief description, would you *buy* it?
  > Is this a fair representation of the work?
  > Is the length appropriate?
  > Is there a (different) quotation I should use?
  > Is there sufficient detail?
  > Does the tone match that of the work?
  > How does it compare with other book jackets?

  Basically, this is an advertisement for your work; make sure you show yourself to best effect.

CHAPTER TWENTY:

BEING A WRITER

Take a look back and reflect on how far you've come. By now, you have sharpened you talents, mastered your craft, and amassed quite a portfolio; you should be truly proud. However... it's not over! Not by a long shot. You're a writer now, and that will never leave you. The tricky part though is to stay with it, so that *you* never leave *it*. Continuing to practice your art consistently can prove to be the most difficult lesson you'll have to learn as a writer. Particularly for those of you taking a class, the risk is extremely high that you, with every intention of returning at some point in the future, will put aside your writing when it is no longer required course material. The only response to this is simple: don't.

Being a writer takes willpower and discipline. Even for those who believe that writing isn't a choice but a necessity, sitting down to put words on a page requires an exertion and a mindfulness that are often elusive. The result? We blow it off, promising ourselves that we'll come back to it, finish it later, start over again when we have the time. We're lazy procrastinators, finding even laundry or wall-watching preferable to taking that seat at our desk and writing down some words. And what's worse is that the longer we put it off, the more likely we are to keep on putting it off; and, while writing is an art we never forget, being in the habit of writing is quite easily forgotten. Once we're out of practice, it often proves burdensome to resume, and so we leave it behind. Again, the only response to this is simple: don't.

Whether you have worked with a class or worked independently, now is the time to forge allegiances with other writers. You need each other. Even if you are one of the few self-motivated souls capable of maintaining your good habits, consider forming relationships with fellow authors. There are several ways to do this. The easiest route to take, if you are in a class, is to turn to the people sitting on either side of you and exchange phone numbers and email addresses. However, if you prefer (or are flying solo), go to your library and post an announcement calling for fellow writers interested in starting a writers' group. It is, of course, also possible to find writers' groups online; however, meeting in person, or at least communicating one-to-one, greatly increases the chances that you'll continue. No matter how you do it, consider establishing some sort of regular meeting with like-minded writers; you can provide each other with much needed support, critiques, and–perhaps most importantly–discipline.

The most dangerous time for a writer is often immediately following the completion of a work (or collection of works). There is usually a dull time that spans the final revision of your manuscript, its publication, and the beginning of a new work. And then, of course, there's the enthusiasm-dampening process of submitting your work–hearing back from agents and publishers can be the most gut-wrenching, ego-blasting experience you've ever endured. This is when you need the help that only a fellow writer can offer. Who else will understand the feeling of sending your prized possession, your creation, your beloved baby, out into the world only to hear back that the world ain't interested? Writers need writers; that's the long and the short of it, so get yourself some.

Beyond that, whether you write every day or every week, whether you write in the morning or at night, or whether you write on the computer or on paper, doesn't really matter. Ideally, you will have gotten into a groove, so that, say, early morning before your kids are up or late at night after your roommate goes to sleep is your time to write, but as long as you have a pattern you're comfortable with, you're in good shape. If, however, writing becomes a practice that bends around to accommodate every other demand life places on you, you could be in trouble. Don't allow your writing to get squeezed in–or worse, squeezed out. Take yourself and your writing seriously; if you don't, who will?

EXERCISES

1. As a writer, you're going to need a lot of encouragement. These exercises are designed to help find and establish the support necessary to keep you motivated.
    - It is essential for you to find some corps of writers if you plan to continue. One of the best ways to do this is to start your own writers' group. Find local, like-minded authors in your area by posting signs at your library, community college, theater, or grocery store. You could also submit an announcement to your local paper, calling for fellow writers. However you form your group, aim to discuss and decide upon the following considerations at your first meeting:
        Where will you meet?
        How often will you meet (weekly, bi-weekly, monthly)?
        How long will meetings run?
        Who will lead the sessions, or will the position rotate?
        How will you handle digressions from writings?
        Will there be specific assignments to work on?
        Who will provide topics and/or prompts for writings?

How will sessions be organized?
Will writings be shared orally, emailed, or printed?
How will critiques be provided?
How will you handle revisions?
How large a group do you want?
How/ will new members be included?

Establishing guidelines early will save much aggravation and potential discomfort later on, so be clear in your group's intentions. There is, of course, no right way to conduct writers' group meetings; the important thing is that you find a group you're comfortable with, and then stick with it. It helps to be flexible, but do discuss what your policy will be when people get off-track (with the inevitable discussions about town politics, kids' schools, or angry spouses) because, rest assured, this *will* happen. Try rotating as much as possible, as well, as this will offer everyone a sense of inclusion as well as responsibility for the group.

- If you choose to keep in contact electronically with classmates or specific, like-minded peers, there are courtesies that should be extended and guidelines that should be established at the outset. No one likes being barraged with hundreds of pages of unedited attachments, right? As with the writers' group (see above), it is important to set some ground rules right from the start. Consider doing the following:

    Requiring that all work be proofread (even first drafts)
    Limiting word, line, or page counts per exchange
    Establishing turn-around times
    Discussing formats for critiques and reviews
    Designating who will be receiving exchanged works
    Forbidding exchanges with non-members
    Prohibiting the forwarding of any works
    Mandating copyrights on all exchanged material
    Selecting assignments for each other
    Determining when, exactly, you will communicate
    Deciding whether all interchanges will be electronic

Remember that the point of a writers' group is to support you in your writing; if your group becomes an impediment to your writing by either taking up too much of your time in critiquing others' work or by not providing you with the kind of feedback and motivation you need, consider finding a different support system. Ideally, your group will provide you with the structure and assistance you need to continue without causing undue distractions and disruptions.

2. As an alternative to these more personal routes, there are a variety of internet formats available to aspiring writers, as well. Consider these formats if maintaining distance or anonymity is critical to you.

    - A multitude of websites exists for the writer who either can't or chooses not to find a more intimate group of peers. Although these sites each have their own style and instructions, they share certain characteristics that may prove desirable to you. Websites can be very freeing to those who are uncomfortable sharing their work with a familiar audience. Or, for authors working on memoirs in which subjects and characterizations may prove hurtful (or harmful) to certain individuals, anonymity may be the only available option. Keep in mind however, that true privacy is not only not guaranteed, it is expressly unavailable. Once your work is posted on or shared through a website, it is in the public domain. Copywriting is critical here, in order to protect the authenticity of your authorship. Websites can be extremely validating, and they can offer a wealth of information about publishers, agents, slams, readings, journals, etc.; you simply must remember to approach them with caution.

- Another electronic option you may want to consider is blogging. Although this format is not actually publishing your work, it *is* advertising it in advance. On your blog, you may choose to post your work (either in its entirety or in clips), you may ask for opinions on revising, formatting, and publishing, and you may create a link to your email where readers can respond and offer commentary. A blog will be most helpful after you've completed your work and are looking for guidance about how to continue. And, in turn, you may inspire others to pursue their dream of becoming a writer. However, because your readers will be unscreened and at liberty to respond any way they like, you may end up getting some undeservedly nasty comments; and while this is excellent practice for potentially hostile professional reviews in the future, it can be seriously discouraging to your craft and damaging to your ego. So, undertake blogging only if you are technically savvy enough to manage it and thick-skinned enough to endure it. Of course, as with all electronic venues, before you embark, make sure you've protected your original materials with a copyright.

EPILOGUE

Whether you write out of pure inspiration or sheer discipline, putting your words on a page is a liberating and joyous undertaking. The exercises contained in this book have been designed to enhance this experience, and with luck, they have. Each has been tried, tested, and revised with you, the evolving writer, in mind. Keep any that were particularly helpful and return to them from time to time; a little practice never hurts, after all. Even the most accomplished writers can still improve their craft; and no good writer allows himself to grow stale.

Above all else, I hope this text allowed you to explore the talents that lie within yourself. Maybe you knew or suspected that they were there all along, or maybe you surprised yourself with their revelation. No matter what, I hope that you were inspired by your capabilities and your growth, and I hope this text helped you in your discovery. Often, all it takes to get going is the right prompt: a suggestion, an idea, or a simple pat on the back. It was the intention of this book to provide all three. Writers are people, too, and we can all use a bit of assistance now and again.

It could be that publication is just ahead, and you will be one of the lucky, talented writers who smoothly coast into fame and great reviews; more realistically, you will turn down a few dead ends before arriving at your destination. But regardless of how you get there, remember that writing isn't only about hitting the finish line. Writing is the lovely Sunday drive, as well. Look around and enjoy it.

Now put down this book and go write.

INDEX

A
Agent, 17, 18, 19, 22, 23, 25, 27, 29-31, 41, 58, 61, 78, 79, 82, 84
Audience, 61-64
Autobiography, 25
Author bio, 78-79

B
Body language, 28, 29
Book jacket, 78-80

C
Character, 17-20
Character sketch, 3, 6, 21
Chronology, 41
Clarity, 7, 74, 75
Cliché, 10, 11, 69
Cohesion, 74
Communication, 15, 28, 61, 63
Concrete, 5, 6, 9, 30, 49-51
Conflict, 21-23
Convention, 30
Conversation, 2, 5, 15, 18, 28, 38, 45, 46, 59, 63
Copyright, 78, 83, 84

D
Dialogue, 2, 16, 26, 27, 41, 68
Diction, 45
Draft, 11, 73, 74, 80, 83
Drama, 14, 21, 25, 26, 29, 33, 53, 57, 63

E
Epigraph, 80
Figure, 13, 19, 21, 25, 26, 49, 58, 62

F
Flashback, 41-43

G
Genre, 21, 25, 35, 66, 67, 75
Grammar, 74

H
Habit, 5, 14, 41, 42, 46, 81
Hero, 13, 30, 55, 56, 58

I
Identity, 35

Image, 3, 6, 10, 11, 14, 18, 22, 34, 37, 39, 46, 47, 49, 50, 55, 59, 62, 63, 64, 71, 72
Imagination, 15
Inspiration, 2, 79, 85
Interlocutor, 2, 45, 62, 63
Irony, 57-60

J
Journal, 53, 67, 79, 84

L
Literal, 49
Literature, 2, 41, 42, 44, 50, 53, 54, 57, 61
Lyric, 49

M
Manuscript, 77-80, 82
Memoir, 17, 18, 21, 23, 25, 29, 30, 33, 39, 42, 84
Metaphor, 5, 71
Meter, 76
Monologue, 1, 26, 27, 33
Mood, 9, 18, 22, 72
Motivation, 2, 29-32, 68, 83

N
Narrator, 13, 18, 22, 30, 31, 33, 34, 36, 41, 43, 58, 62
   First-person, 35, 43
   Omnicient, 34
   Retrospective, 34, 43
   Second-person, 33
   Third-person, 35
   Unreliable, 37-40

P
Persona, 1, 14, 25, 27
Perspective, 1, 11, 22, 23, 25, 26, 27, 33, 34, 35, 37, 43, 50, 51, 52
Plot, 14, 17, 18, 21, 22, 23, 27, 30, 31, 35, 39, 41, 43, 54, 57, 62, 68, 80

Poetry, 9, 21, 22, 25, 26, 27, 29, 30, 33, 43, 66, 71, 74, 78
Point of view, 33-36, 37, 39, 51, 52
Prose, 39
Protagonist, 9, 18, 33
Publish, 23, 77, 78, 79, 84

R
Reader, 6, 9, 14, 20, 31, 32, 33, 35, 37, 45, 46, 54, 55, 58, 65, 67, 74, 76, 78, 80, 84
Retrospective, 34, 41, 42, 43
Review, 51, 65-70, 73, 74, 77, 83, 84, 85
Revision, 66, 67, 72, 73-76, 82, 83
Rhythm, 26, 71, 75, 76

S
Scene, 15, 22, 23, 27, 30, 31, 38, 58, 59, 68, 74, 75, 76
Screenplay, 13, 25, 27, 33, 39, 74
Semiotics, 5
Setting, 9-11, 15, 30, 68
Speech, 26, 27, 28, 30, 41, 49, 63
Star, 13, 17, 18, 22, 33, 39
Stock figure, 17
Sub-text, 15, 68, 69
Symbol, 5, 6, 49-52

T
Tension, 21, 22, 23, 28, 31, 38, 41, 42, 58
Time sequence, 41
Title, 10, 68, 69, 71, 77, 78, 79
Tone, 9, 15, 18, 39, 59, 68, 77, 79, 80

W
Writer's block, 2
Writers' group, 55, 67, 76, 82, 83

V
Voice, 1, 13, 15, 23, 25, 26, 27, 33, 34, 35, 36, 39, 43, 61, 62, 66, 80

ABOUT THE AUTHOR

Stephanie Stiles is a professor of English at Dominican College in New York, where she chairs the department and directs the Creative Writing Program. Her prize-winning poetry, as well as her fiction and non-fiction, have appeared in various contemporary anthologies and journals. Her first novel will be published in 2011. She received her doctorate in nineteenth century British literature from New York University, and now lives with her husband, son, and baby daughter in Northern New Jersey.

www.ingramcontent.com/pod-product-compliance
Lightning Source LLC
Chambersburg PA
CBHW031555300426
44111CB00006BA/318